ABDUCTED & FURIOUS

How I Fought Back and How You Can Too

A TRUE STORY

BY **LISA O'HARA**

*Janet,
thank you for the reading) — it really helped me. Thank you for your support! Lisa O'Hara*

Abducted & Furious: How I Fought Back and How You Can Too

Copyright © 2020 by Lisa O'Hara

All rights reserved. No part of this book may be reproduced or transmitted in any form or by any means, electronic or mechanical, including photocopying, recording, or by any information storage and retrieval system without the written permission of the author, except where permitted by law.

ISBN: 978-1-7345609-0-9

Editing & Cover Design: George Verongos

Foreword

The reasons I wrote this book are three fold. First, to write about my experiences, second to raise awareness, and third, to help anyone that has been abducted by ETs or the military. I wanted to be able to share the information from my spirit guides on how to fight back against being abducted to as many people as possible, as quickly as possible. As more and more people awaken to the truth, they will need resources. We need more people to speak out, but we also need tools to fight back.

Once I found tools, used them and they worked, I knew that I could not keep them to myself. I had to find my people and share the tools. Sounds easy, but it is difficult in a world where no one talks about being abducted by ETs.

Finding a UFO group is hard enough but finding a person who has negative ET/abduction experiences is even harder. I think this is by design.

So, with some trepidation, fear, and wondering what in the heck I had gotten myself into, I decided to forge on and write this book.

I have been told it is not done to point people to other books in your book. But, I'm doing it anyway because it's the right thing to do. In the back of this book there will be a listing of the books/tools I used, plus an outline on how to use the tools. These tools will help anyone who is unhappy to find out that they, also, are an abductee and will show them how to fight back and reclaim their lives. We have to help each other, even if it's not done.

What if, instead of erasing our memories, we have personalities that were created/splintered off because of the high-intensity trauma in our lives; an "alter?" This would explain why we have no memories of these events that we go through each night because our current personality is asleep while the alternate personality performs tasks. It would also explain why the sleeping personality gets the stun gun. It's to keep the sleeping personality asleep.

Some of you might think to yourself, *There's no proof*. This is true. And, that I don't have a lot of photos. This is also true. Not realizing I would write a book, I did not take a lot of photos. Now that I need them for this book, I don't find bruises on my body anymore. I never get bruises and I believe it's because I have eliminated the majority of the abductors. If you are considering writing a book, I urge you to not be like me, take those pictures. But I want to say that all abductees know the truth. The abductions are real, proof or no proof.

Acknowledgements

Thank you Gwen Farrell, who took my document and edited it for the first draft. It was a learning experience for me.

I want to thank my husband, Bob, who was supportive during the hours I spent writing and helped me find the right word when I needed it.

George Verongos, all abductees know that safety is an illusion. I have not felt safe in a very long time. However, while working with you, I felt it again. I have been enjoying and cherishing the precious gift of feeling safe in this process of book writing and self-publishing. Your knowledge, patience, humor and guidance has been amazing and I'm so grateful for you. Thank you so much for everything.

Thank you Terry Lovelace for your support, and for pointing me in the direction of George Verongos.

Thank you Stewart Swerdlow and Janet Mourglia-Swerdlow for writing your books. I found them when I needed them, and they have given me great hope for the future.

I want to thank everyone who has the courage to write a book about ET/military abductions. Thank you!

This book is for humanity and all abductees who suffer in silence every day.

TABLE OF CONTENTS

Introduction: Take back your power!... 1
Chapter 1: My Story: What am I? 3
Chapter 2: Mediumship..5
Chapter 3: Abductions Revealed 9
Chapter 4: Tools the Medium Used In Addition to Meditation and Healing.. 11
Chapter 5: The Loophole: Best and Highest Good........................ 13
Chapter 6: Noticing the Clues 15
Chapter 7: Seeing is Believing... 17
Chapter 8: Remote Viewers and Pandora's Box 19
Chapter 9: Beware of Remote Viewers 23
Chapter 10: Time Bending 25
Chapter 11: Programming 29
Chapter 12: Self-Care... 31
Chapter 13: Meditation 33
Chapter 14: Pyramids 35
Chapter 15: Clearing a Room... 37
Chapter 16: Rocks and Crystals 41
Chapter 17: Clues 43
Chapter 18: Dreams... 49
Chapter 19: Abductors are MIMICS... 53
Chapter 20: Fear 55
Chapter 21: Implant in Eyeball 57
Chapter 22: Teaching/Sharing These Tools with Others 59
Chapter 24: Searching for Help 61
Chapter 25: Knowing You are on the Right Track......................... 65
Chapter 26: The Tools aka The Big Guns 67

Chapter 27: What I do, Step by Step 77
Chapter 28: What I've Learned About Dreams 93
Chapter 29: What I've Learned About Meditation 95
Chapter 30: Abductors/ETs are Narcissists! 97
Chapter 31: Deceptions of the ETs/Military 105
Chapter 32: My Experiences 2017 109
Chapter 31: My Experiences 2018 123
Chapter 32: My Experiences 2019 165
Chapter 33: Learn from Me 203
Chapter 34: Don't Give Up and Let's Help Each Other 205
Chapter 35: A Few Thoughts 207
Resources 211
How to Build Your Own Portable Copper Pyramid 213
Level the Playing Field with Negative ETs Handout 215

Introduction
Take back your power!

When I discovered in 2017 that I was being abducted by Grays every single night, I freaked out. My world was turned upside down and I felt scared to death and unsafe. It made me question the bucolic feeling of Earth. There is a safety that we all feel being here. Nothing is perfect, but we can often feel relatively safe. We feel we can pin down the fears and see them—robbers, criminals, etc. But, when we know something is happening to us that we don't understand, or that we can't see or remember—what a helpless feeling! Those of us in this position know well how they felt when they first found out. When those feelings of fear wore off, I felt outraged and furious. I was so angry that they had the nerve to take me, it served as a catalyst for my journey to figure out how to stop it.

I have since discovered that I get abducted several times a night. At the time I discovered this, I was being mentored by a psychic medium to learn how to become a practicing medium, how to connect to spirits on the other side, how to do protections, how to turn the connection to the spirits on and off, make it a business etc. After about six months, I knew mediumship was not for me. I wanted more. Spirits and the like do come to me and I help them when I can, but this is not my main focus. I am not a practicing medium.

I spent almost two years working with that medium to stop the abductions and we tried everything. The ETs/abductors kept coming back through any and all of her "protections."

Meditation and healing techniques helped me feel better and I also received guidance from my spirit guides, but not one thing the medium did or told me to do stopped the abductions from taking place. The abductions continued despite everything we were doing to stop them from happening!

What I didn't know at the time was that while the medium was trying to help me, she couldn't with just her tools. **Her tools did not work by themselves. Meditation and healing were half of the puzzle.**

Finally, in November 2018 in desperation, I revisited some healing books I had bought in 2017 and was ushered back to by my spirit guides. I had nothing to lose, so, I read them.

These books, while esoteric to me the year before, now made sense. It must have been the right time. I had the right amount of experience to see these books and the tools within them and make the connections to use them against abductions of all types, ET or military. These tools worked! **These tools are the other half of the puzzle.**

To rid yourself of abductions by the military or ET, you need **meditation, healing, and the tools within these pages**. Meditation and healing is positivity and the tools eliminate negativity. This is the yin/yang. This is why we need both. Heal first with meditation to obtain downloads, information you need, etc., second, rid yourself of negativity, then third, self-healing.

I wrote this book to help and inform as many abductees as possible who are having **negative** experiences, whether by ETs or military abductors. I have not had any success in finding people like me with negative ET experiences.

Here is my story, the tools I use, and the procedures I use. Let's unleash our fury on **all** abductors, ET and military.

Chapter 1
My Story: What am I?

As a child I had strange experiences. I had dreams that came true, daydreams that I would have daily for a week that would come true (that's how I thought of them as a child: A daydream that would come unbidden and that would not go away). This was remote viewing, although I didn't know it at the time. I also had nightmares, was afraid of the dark as all kids are and just knew there were monsters under my bed. Once, when I was 11 and living in Alabama, I saw what looked like a bright white circle that followed me into bed. I remember yelling "Oh no, oh no!" I did not understand my fear of it.

Life continued on. When I was 28, I started having night terrors. I was married at the time and if I went to bed before my husband did, as soon as he crossed the threshold from another room to the bedroom, I would sit up and scream like someone was killing me. All I could remember was a black rectangle. For years this plagued me. Therapy for this didn't help. Also that same year, a friend at work told me about a book by Budd Hopkins called *Intruders*. I read part of it but became so frightened; I remember throwing the book across the room. I stopped reading it and tried to forget the parts I had read.

In 1992, I separated from my husband and I started sleepwalking. I would wake up crouched on the edge of my bed peering into the closet or running down the hallway that led to the bedrooms. In desperation, I asked for it all to stop. I was living alone, had sketchy neighbors and two jobs. I could not deal with one extra thing. It stopped.

In 2011, there I was watching *American Idol* all alone, and being a person who cannot carry a tune I was saying in my head probably 1000 times, *I wish I could sing, I wish I could sing.* I thought that I was alone in my head. Suddenly, someone also inside of my head, with a male authoritative voice said, "Be grateful for the gifts you do have." I thought to myself, *What gifts?*

In 2012 I had started meditating and trying to figure out what I was or what the "gift" I had was. Was I an intuitive? Psychic? I began reading books and felt guided to a book about how to tell if you're a medium. I read it. I thought it was vague and so, while thinking to myself, I thought, *Well, I could be a medium but I'm not married to being a medium.* Immediately, some knocking on the wall started happening. Was that a sign? Maybe I was a medium?

Chapter 2
Mediumship

After meditating a lot, I started to sense more—I could smell things—like pickles inside my car, or see accidents on the road that happened at some point. I would see the aftermath in my head as if I was in the accident, like I was reliving it.

I meditated and asked to know the name of my spirit guide and also to know my purpose. I learned that my guide's name is Koreg and my purpose is to be a beacon of light. What? Huh? I had no idea what that meant at the time but now I think it means—showing people the way.

In 2014, I found a group on the book of faces that had a medium in it and she said she mentored those of us who wanted to build our skills for mediumship. She was a very strange lady. We tried several times to connect for a mentoring and it never worked out. I like to think it was my guides protecting me. But, her equipment would stop working each and every time we tried to connect via Skype. This woman wrote a book and I found out the hard way that her "followers" were all "yes men," there to promote her book only. She deleted any comments she didn't like. She told me that I unfriended her. I did not. Fortunately for me, there was a guy in there who said he would be happy to mentor me. So, we started an email exchange. At first being very green and naïve, I thought I was just trying to learn about ghosts/the dead/spirits/etc. and behind the veil meant cool stuff. I feel so dumb now.

Since my mother passed away in September 2014, I explored my anger at my mother. I had a difficult relationship with her. She had narcissistic tendencies and I had learned to be careful around her. I could never be myself. When she passed I was so angry. Koreg told me, prior to her death, that I would go through a huge release. I kept waiting for it and wondering what that meant.

Unfortunately for me, and probably for you, guides are cryptic and do not give you the answer or their reasons for wanting you to do something. I've learned to just do whatever it is they are advising me to do and wait for the answer. You will find out why, but not on your timetable. Or, it might make sense years later. My anger at my mother was my release. My mentor from the Facebook medium group reminded me that the anger was a catalyst. I raged at her and asked her why. Why didn't she let me in? Why did she force me to limit my interactions with her and keep my distance? I was told that she was on HER mission to make me into the person I needed to be for MY mission. Knowing this, all of my anger disappeared because there's just no arguing with that.

I was unsure where to go from here. But, how to get started as a medium? What does one do? Are there teachers? Mentors? Finding one was a challenge. Years went by and my spirit guides kept telling me to have patience and to continue with meditation. I did as I was told. But, I was frustrated with the pace.

In December 2016, while at the hair salon, there was another customer there who let us all know that her boss was a medium. I was excited. I had been meditating and asking for help to find a mentor, a teacher. That was exactly what I was looking for.

In January 2017, I went to that medium and started studying to become a practicing medium myself, because at our first meeting, this medium told me she knew I was like her, a medium. I first went to her to find out about my mother, since she passed away in 2014. I went every week or two and diligently did my homework to learn the trade of a practicing medium. I did really want to help people and I felt this was the only way to do that. I was all in. I received messages regularly from my spirit guides. One I received on January 31, 2017 was: "We are preparing you. Not just for mediumship but to be a warrior." I did not know what this meant at the time.

While learning how to be a practicing medium I learned about "setting sacred space," the "violet flame of Saint Germain," protections, i.e., using a mirror shield. I did experiments on negative people and pulled up various shields to protect me from the energy vampires and narcissists, which I have had a problem with my whole life. I learned about energy surrounding us and drawing people to us. I took every class my medium offered, angelic symbols, introduction to energy healing, energy shares, everything. Every night I set my sacred space and protections per my medium's instructions. My husband called it "My Manifesto" because I would read it out loud each night before bed. I read everything I could about setting sacred space and I practiced it diligently.

Chapter 3
Abductions Revealed

One night, in 2017, I was talking to my spirit guide, Koreg, and felt a negative presence in my room. Very negative. I asked Koreg, "Who is in my room? What is that negative feeling?" He said, "It's ETs. They took all of your eggs and this is the reason you don't have children and they're here to take you." Up to this point, I had no idea that I was ever taken. I do not have children and never had the ticking clock. Was this the reason?

Therein starteth my wild ride with knowing about abductions. Of course, I was angry, frightened and in disbelief. It took me a few weeks to get used to the idea. I told my husband, Bob, about it. He poo-pooed it. Strangely, that made me feel better and safe. I had the time to get used to it at my own pace. I needed to be grounded.

I started Googling anything about ETs and people being taken and what they did about it. I needed ideas. I tried everything I could find.

I continued with the medium. Now that I knew about the ETs taking me, I needed help figuring out what to do about it.

I was scared to death to sleep and stayed up all night keeping watch. I got some cameras that looked like picture frames, to catch them in the act. I watched obsessively for the ETs to show up, moved around my house in the middle of the night and felt exhausted, but they still managed to take me each night. The picture frame "nanny cams" were motion activated. However, as you might expect, my nanny cam mysteriously stopped working each time they came. Because I didn't think I should tell my husband about it, I told him I was trying to catch ghosts.

The medium had the idea that I had abduction contracts that I chose before my birth here on Earth that needed to be cancelled. So, we started working on breaking those contracts.

Chapter 4
Tools the Medium Used In Addition to Meditation and Healing

The tools of the medium's trade were: meditation and healing.

For ridding me of what she considered to be a soul contract, or ET contract, we tried everything from: removing myself from soul contracts, healing from ET contracts, setting sacred space and protections each night, clearing Akashic Records, clearing my space, putting salt out, showering with salt, being loud, commanding and demanding my right to FREE WILL before bed, stating my sovereignty before bed, stating my right to FREE WILL, asking for whatever was in my highest and best good. None of that worked.

The abductions continued despite everything we tried. And I was motivated. I wanted it to work and I stayed with her working on it, diligently. I also frantically searched the internet for anything else I could use. For two years, nothing she did for abductions stopped them. It was as if I was just saying nonsensical words.

The medium claimed that the ETs never messed with her because she was so tough and the reason I couldn't stop them was because I wasn't being tough enough, demanding enough. I tried harder.

Chapter 5
The Loophole: Best and Highest Good

The medium kept using the phrase, "Highest and best good. Best and highest healing." She was under the impression that this was my journey and I chose this experience. I was not convinced I would choose something like this. I felt she was blaming me for being abducted. At the time I just tried harder.

However, **this is not our fault**. She also felt that I was being a victim and choosing to be a victim because of these abductions. She wanted me to know my own power, but what I discovered was that she was teaching me to give away my power by using "best and highest good."

It turns out that best and highest good is something all New Age people use. But it doesn't work because we are giving away our power. It sounds good, like we're choosing "best and highest good" but when we ask for BEST and HIGHEST GOOD, **who are we asking? WHO are we letting choose our best and highest good? WHO decides** what is in our best and highest good? **Not us**! But, it's a loophole that everyone uses. **STOP USING THIS!**

Chapter 6
Noticing the Clues

At some point, I started to notice something strange about my freshly laundered clothing and other clothing I wear more than once because I don't sweat in my clothes and I shower regularly. I was in my laundry room getting some clothes that Bob, my husband, had folded after I had washed them. And, my clothes smelled funny. They smelled like a combination of body odor and feet. I smelled a bunch of my clothing and it all smelled the same— B.O. and feet. I assumed it was because I was not putting in enough laundry detergent.

So, I put all of those smelly clothes in the hamper and the next day I washed them all again with extra laundry detergent. I then put those clothes away and everything was fine. No problem. Then, it happened again, the smelly clothes problem, when the day before everything smelled fine coming out of the dryer.

The clothes were all my favorite shirts. Since I have two cats and the cat boxes are in the laundry room, I figured that was the problem, so I resolved to make a beeline for when the clothes came out of the dryer and hang them up. Everything seemed fine, until I placed a shirt (my favorite) on the counter in my bathroom to wear the next day. The next day, it smelled like B.O. and feet. I hadn't worn it and it wasn't in the laundry room. This kept happening. After that, I started putting all dried clothing away immediately into the closet, but I would leave my workout gear on the counter.

Interestingly, I then had a dream that I was wearing a bright neon orange exercise top. That same workout top had been on the counter in my bathroom. It was then I realized that whenever I smelled the B.O./feet combination on my clothes it was because I put those clothes on when I was abducted.

Now, each time I get up, I smell my clothes and I know if I've been abducted. I figure it's the environment that is causing the smell as well as the length of time I'm in that environment.

I brush my teeth before bed but invariably found most mornings that I had plaque. It was strange. I also wear a night guard on my bottom teeth to protect them from grinding. At first I thought I missed a spot when I brushed the night before. But, I kept finding plaque even though I checked before going to bed to make sure there were no spots of plaque after brushing. At the time, I was voraciously reading the book called *MILABS: Military Mind Control and Alien Abduction* by Dr. Helmut Lammer & Marion Lammer. The Lammers talked about drinking something, in the military abductions. It made me think: *AHA! This is why I am finding plaque on my teeth after sleeping. I'm going somewhere and eating something.* I didn't know why though.

Chapter 7
Seeing is Believing

It was a night in September 2017, that I had a run in with a recycle bin (a tall one) and cut the top of my right leg near the knee. That same week, at my medium's office after my recycle bin encounter, the medium told me about her acupuncturist, who had an office near her office. She said he was very intuitive, so I went to him because I wanted to see who was taking me, since I could only feel their negativity but couldn't see them. I told him what I wanted, to see the ETs.

He did what acupuncturists do, put in needles, painful but effective acupuncture, and lo and behold, that night my leg was throbbing and I saw an ET. It was a Praying Mantis who appeared by my bed. Telepathically, she told me that she knew my leg was hurting and she begged me to let her take me to her ship to fix it. She gave me the feeling of warmth and motherliness. I struggled with it. Being an empath, I wanted to give her what she wanted but...not enough to get on a ship. She was tall and greenish. I'm pretty sure she took me anyway and I realized later that there was a beacon in my leg and it called her. We all have implants, y'all.

I regularly find bumps on my body that are not pimples but are left behind by what look like stun gun marks. They are sometimes very small ¼ inch in length, or an inch in length. They are parallel to each other, like a stun gun prong would attach to the skin. Sometimes they are vertical indicators that the stun gun prongs were vertically placed on the skin. The bumps have a hole in them. I've found that these bumps seem to be the aftermath of a stun, which renders me unconscious and the little lumps that I can scratch out but not squeeze out, since they are not pimples are actually the burned skin of the prongs that are used by the ETs. The bumps are not milia. I have those too, but milia, for me, cannot be excised, even by scratching at them. I've tried, because I do get milia. These bumps are different. If you squeeze them, they will get inflamed and if you scratch them, a little hard, white lump comes out. I have not had them tested but they are organic/biological and disintegrate after a short time. As an experiment, because why not, I was using rare earth magnets and rubbing them all over my body—to kill all of the implants. I don't know if it worked, but I enjoyed the thought of annoying the ETs immensely.

Chapter 8
Remote Viewers and Pandora's Box

In August 2017, I read a book called *Psychic Warrior* by David Morehouse. I was very interested in his stories about remote viewing as he learned how to do this in the military.

Coordinate Remote Viewing description from the website *Davidmorehouse.com*:

"Our online course will guide you through the protocols and theory behind Coordinate Remote Viewing. It is your first step into understanding our connection to the matrix of all things. As you begin to practice and step into your mind's eye you quickly experience a greater understanding that we are more than our physical bodies. You will go from *believing to knowing*. Coordinated Remote Viewing is defined by the Defense Department of the United States as the learned ability to transcend time and space, to view people, places and things remote in time and space and to gather information on the same. Students learn to enter an altered state of consciousness, receive a set of encrypted coordinates, produce an ideogram (the first graphic representation of the target site), and decode the ideogram..."

So, I purchased David Morehouse's online class on Coordinate Remote Viewing (CRV) through Soundstrue.com. I started it. I did my CRV several times until one time I smelled flowers, like lavender. I thought it might be my perfume/deodorant or my imagination.

The second time I did Coordinate Remote Viewing, I had an unusual experience. There I was, concentrating on the target and trying to feel the signal line when I felt like I moved to a different room—I was in an office—not a very plush office, but one that would be in a nonprofit (I used to work with several). There was white flooring tiles, a computer in front of me with a CRT (computer monitor, the huge boxy kind) and men all around me in white shirts (think business shirts). I could smell coffee. I do not drink coffee and neither does my husband. I was in an office chair and these men in business clothing were all around me drinking coffee from cups. Then I heard someone say "Oh, there you are!" That scared me.

After that CRV session was over, I started hearing popping, thunking and cracking and it followed me from room to room. I started making the connection between CRV and remote viewers. It was as if I had opened a door and whoever was looking for me had found me and now, sounds followed me wherever I was in my house. After that, I was plagued by remote viewers everywhere I went, outside, in my car, in my house. And by plagued, I mean hounded by noises that sound like your house is settling or the wind is going through your house—a huge wind, making everything creak. Yes, houses creak and settle. If it's windy outside, yes, that might be your house creaking, and settling but if you are sitting around your house and it sounds like the thunking, cracking, and snapping noises follow you from room to room, then, those sounds are not normal, they are remote viewers. If you feel the room change in pressure, that is also a remote viewer. It was so bad that I joined a Facebook remote viewer group and begged for help. I didn't get any help, instead I was ridiculed and judged for being paranoid.

I eventually, bought the Coordinate Remote Viewing class online from *Davidmorehouse.com* because it was the second half of the Coordinated Remote Viewing course from Sounds True. I took his classes because I read his book but also because he has a very nice voice and takes you through it step by step. I learn best in this manner. I am a linear learner. I thought at first that I would prefer Coordinate Remote Viewing because it's very structured and I like structure. I can learn it if I can see it in a linear manner. I read other books on remote viewing and they were very technical. While I am a technical person with computers, with new subjects, I prefer the step-by-step method. Help me understand our goals and I will be able to do it.

Extended Remote Viewing description from the website of *Davidmorehouse.com*:

"Extended Remote Viewing or ERV is designed to guide students through the application of a hybrid form of Remote Viewing. It is knowledge of "knowing" based instruction. This means that the basic ERV student has moved to a new level of understanding what we call 'the matrix of our creation;' accepting one's concepts as being 'knowledge' and not merely 'belief' based. ERV is an experience that Remote Viewing students call 'Learning to Fly' because of the overwhelming sensation of free flight and movement felt during the session."

In June 2019, I decided to try Extended Remote Viewing (ERV) because (1) it seemed like I should (probably a nudge from my guides) and (2) it was less structured than CRV. Since I had already purchased this ERV class, I decided to go ahead and try it. I had to make a conscious choice, with trepidation, knowing what Pandora's box I opened last time.

With this specific class, there are precise instructions to keep you safe. For the exercises with the targets, there are specific instructions regarding what you're supposed to see and record. Without giving this class away—I'll give you a few things to help you understand my experience using this technique. First, you listen to music that allows your mind to clear. Second, you use an eye mask to keep distractions at bay. Third, you create a code word that will take you back to your safe spot if necessary. There are other steps, but to understand my experiences, this is all you need to know.

The first ERV session, I made some mistakes and missed the target because, since it was my first time, I was going through the steps in my mind and unwittingly used the code word and ended up back at my safe place. I then had to go back and I tried not to overthink things. I did not end up at the target. I did end up in a nice place, with a farm, with a woman making dinner. The instructions said to list the time of day and other things I can't remember. Since it was a farm and I didn't see any clocks, I did what I could. I came back and found that I did not hit the target, but I had a good experience.

My second experience with ERV was not a good one. Here's what happened: I had my eye mask on and I was the only person in the room when I felt someone or something touch my eyes over my mask. I saw only blackness after that. I need to get back to it, but …. Clearly someone doesn't want me to experience ERV. I personally think it opens things up in your mind. So, that's all the reason I need—try to stop me!

Chapter 9
Beware of Remote Viewers

Speaking of remote viewers, I have figured out what they sound like and who they are. I can't see them but I can hear them.

- A thunk (like thunking a watermelon) = **Human**.
- A crack = **ET**.
- A snap = Invisible Beings.

How did I find this out? I asked them. I do admit to sometimes yelling at them about how they would feel if they were watched this closely, but I also ask them questions. The humans talked to me and said that it's their job and they have bills to pay. The ETs never talk, so at first it was just two types of remote viewers and I was able to distinguish ETs from humans. Then, a snap noise started up and I was told by my guides that these were called "invisible beings." I don't know what these are but they might be watching you.

In my experience, remote viewers are invisible negative entities. This is not to say that every remote viewer is negative, but my experiences have been with only the negative ones. They can feel negative or neutral. I have never felt a positive remote viewer and consider them all negative, even the neutral remote viewers. My feeling is that if you're not with me, you're against me, and I've made that very clear to them by telling them how I feel. I also make sure they know *I know* they're in my house or car, or wherever they appear.

I've started seeing invisible beings a lot outside and inside my house. The air moves around them and they are not completely invisible. You can see something, but not an outline. When I was writing this book, I saw them a lot and heard them because I had taken my computer off the internet, using it standalone and invisible beings were dispatched to my office where I was writing and typing. They all want to know what I'm doing and what I know.

A note about remote viewers. Some are neutral. I have found that neutral does not mean good or in your favor. They are watching you for whatever information they can obtain. They are not benevolent. **Be careful of them.**

You can find remote viewers in your car too. I live in Arizona, so I have water bottles in my car full or some empty at any given time. When remote viewers come into my car, the water bottles crack, because of the pressure changes that the remote viewers cause in the environment. This is called "the membrane" (which I learned in ERV) and when the pressure changes **anywhere,** unless you're on a plane and it's supposed to happen, a remote viewer is nearby. I believe the noises I hear—cracking, thunking or snapping—are also the membrane of the various entities. I've noticed that the air pressure changes when someone or something shows up in my car. This happens also in my house.

There are many types of remote viewing. There are many teachers, David Morehouse, Lyn Buchanan, to name a few. Lyn Buchanan has a new class that just came out called Associative Remote Viewing which is an online course at crviewer.com. I suggest to all of you that you learn the remote viewing skill. It is very helpful and can help you unlock what the ETs/military have been doing to you without your knowledge. Find out the truth with remote viewing.

Chapter 10
Time Bending

Time bending is the manipulation of timelines. I live in one timeline that I share with you, the reader. There is more than one timeline. Time bending is taking me from my timeline, moving me to another timeline for an arbitrary length of time on that timeline, and returning me to our own timeline so that anyone else on our timeline can't even see that I was gone. Usually, the only thing that can be noticed is a slight discontinuity when returning to our shared timeline. These time bends are not like missed time where you know you're supposed to be somewhere and now it's dark and time has passed, it's very different. Here are some examples that I have uncovered, where time bending was used.

I have been taken from my car while driving, three times. I hate being taken out of my car like that. So dangerous! The last time I got taken from my car, I was merging onto a freeway! I drive a stick shift. I don't know where I go or who takes me. But they put me back at about the same time as I left. I know that time bending was used because I'm not doing what I'm supposed to do—which is automatic. For you, it could be that you're sitting at a light and they take you at that second when the light changes. When they put you back, it might be a couple seconds before you were taken. So, it takes a few seconds for you to realize that the light hasn't changed and you start to move as if it has, because for you, it just changed.

In the case of the freeway merge, I was just about to shift into 4th gear and when I was placed back into my car, I was in 3rd gear with my blinker on and I wasn't moving over. I was kind of hanging out on the right side of the road, but not merging, like those people who passively merge, waiting for the road to end.

Time bends happen to me when I'm least expecting it. This situation is so disruptive that I am just trying not to freak out and get killed. It's very dangerous and irresponsible to do this to me.

My car is normal the whole "time" this is happening, it's as if my car has no idea that I was even gone, because in our timeline, I never left.

Night seems to be a prime time for these time bends to happen. For example, I might go to bed around 2 AM and have four hours to sleep but it feels like it's been eight. This used to happen to me when I was younger and working two jobs and had a small amount of time for sleeping. I could not figure out why some four-hour nights would feel long and restful, while others would feel short and I would wake up tired. Other nights I might wake up at the same time, three times or go to bed at 2 AM and wake up at 1:35 AM, nearly ½ hour before I went to bed. The reason I know the time so clearly each time I wake up in my bed is because I have a clock that projects the time on the ceiling in red digital numbers. All I have to do is open my eyes to know the time.

As I was driving to a session with my medium, the sun reflected some glare off the car in front of me. Like the negative of a picture, I could see this weird pattern in my eyes—like a question mark. I mentioned to her in that session that on the night before I had woken up three times. First, in abject terror, but I was in my bed. I woke up a second time, feeling fine and wondering why I was so scared before. Then, I woke up a third time feeling abject terror. However, in the morning, I woke up feeling fine and didn't even really know what happened until I saw her and she told me that she knew I had been poked in the eye.

The medium said that her guides told her that the entities put long needles in my eyes, in the whites, and I could see it coming, hence, the abject terror. This information explained what I saw while driving my car to her office; as I was driving, the sun reflected off a car in front of me and there was glare. She confirmed that someone or something poked me in the eyes with long needles and the pattern I saw was a result of that. She said I had been taken for one and a half years and because of the needles, I felt terror. Since the entity bent time, I was put back in my bed multiple times, maybe to show their power? But, I was also given the feeling of terror.

Because of their ability to manipulate our memory, we can feel like nothing happened and even not remember these important details until we see our medium and they indicate that they know we were poked in the eye and we suddenly remember. The terror I felt from the glare of the sun off that car showed me the marks in my eyes. Since the entities bend time, they were able to put me back right when I left/they took me. So, my life was basically unchanged here in our timeline.

CHAPTER 11
PROGRAMMING

You might not think you are programmed but think about how they get you out of your bed at night. Do you think they carry you? Maybe, but maybe they give you a code word and you put on clothes and leave. This was hard for me to swallow, but it makes sense. What about alien apathy? Don't you think it's strange that you, seeing an ET in your room, don't run screaming? Why don't you hit one? Kick it? The answer is programming.

It's there and if you look at society, programming is everywhere. TV shows used to be called a "show" and now everything on TV is called a "program." This might be paranoia, but what if it's just the way to control you without your knowing? I watch a fun bridal show and in every episode they tell the viewers, "the dress is the most important thing." What about advertising? This is the innocuous stuff. Who are you without your programming? Are your habits programmed? Food for thought.

When I'm remote viewing a "dream" or trying to see what happened during the night and why, I see myself as if I'm watching a movie about myself. If, I was lying down or on an operating table, or in a water tank, I am not seeing through my eyes like I do in real life, I'm seeing a scene with me in it. I remote view to be able to use the information both for my own understanding of what's going on and to use the tools I found against these entities that I see. To eliminate ETs, you have to know who and what you're dealing with. The only way out is through. You have to see yourself in the situation and then use the information that you gain against the ETs. This is why remote viewing is so important.

I have had many dreams/remote views about being programmed. On 2/4/19 I found a spot on the right side of my face, a bump, near the corner of my mouth. Bob, my husband, had the same spot on the left side of his mouth. The remote view revealed surgery in different rooms. They were working on the right side of my brain and the left side of Bob's. The doctors were human. They were fixing our programming and wondering aloud how I keep breaking mine. They went in through our mouths.

On 2/13/19, I woke up with a sty on my right eyelid. I did a remote view to see how I got this. The answer: on a ship. Praying Mantises had my right eye out and they were drilling it. Zzzzt, zzzt, zzzzzt and there was something stuck on my eyelid. I started waking up and flailing around. They said I was getting strong and they weren't sure what to do. They also said I tried to access the eyeball which I can only guess means that they knew that I was doing experiments by first trying to talk to the eyeball implant (I named it Harriet) and later, asking my spirit guides to remove it and such like that. One doctor was a small white/cream colored Praying Mantis or a Grasshopper.

On 2/22/19 I did a remote view and saw this: As a little girl, I was given the code words "Rose Garden." When I heard these words, I was to get up and do what I was told, and when I heard the words a second time, my memory would be erased. The programmer had hooked something up to my head and when it was over, I couldn't remember anything. I went to my bunk and talked to my roommate, who asked what happened and I couldn't remember. She left to go see for herself. Later we all (six to nine kids) left our bodies, held hands, and flew to another galaxy. Being "us" sucked.

CHAPTER 12
SELF-CARE

LaHoChi

LaHoChi is an important tool for dealing with the aftermath of your abduction.

Being abducted is extremely stressful and self-care is so important. LaHoChi is what I use to recover from an abduction. It makes me feel better, it helps me sleep and it gives you a healing, as an added bonus.

What is LaHoChi?

From the LaHoChi.com website:

"LaHoChi is a powerful hands on healing technique that brings in a very high frequency of light. Some unique features of this method include an automatic 'seal of protection' around both the healer and the recipient guarding against low frequency vibrations. This ensures that the healer will not absorb any released energies. LaHoChi features five simple hand positions to heal others and four easy self-healing hand positions so you can work on yourself quickly and thoroughly. This type of healing continuously fills the healer with light so there is never a drain to the healer's energy field. The healing creates permanent shifts in our energy field and continuously propels us toward infinite spiritual perfection. There is no hierarchy of healing abilities or levels. You can be administering healing on yourself in less than ½ hour after receiving this handbook."

You can use LaHoChi to heal yourself and others, but first you will need an attunement, which you can get at www.lahochi.com or from another LaHoChi practitioner. But, I caution you to check out the lahochi.com website first and confirm the cost for both the book/attunement because many practitioners will charge $350 for the class/attunement and it will cost you eight hours of your time because they are teaching you how to heal others first, and yourself second.

For the purposes of this book, I'm asking you to learn how to heal yourself first and others second. At www.lahochi.com, you will receive the PDF of the book and the attunement for a very nominal fee ($100). After receiving your attunement, you will be able to heal yourself and others, even teach others how to use it, what a deal. Take care of yourself!

I use LaHoChi when I wake up after being abducted. Use this healing technique each and every time you get abducted, when you wake up. This is so important.

Many energy healing modalities are intended for healing others. I, myself, have taken Reiki, but didn't really like it all that much. LaHoChi felt like the right healing tool for me. I took a class and was hooked.

I don't know about you, but I wake up suddenly after abduction and then can't sleep afterwards. LaHoChi helps me sleep and as an added bonus I get healed.

CHAPTER 13
MEDITATION

Meditation is an important tool for dealing with abductions. Do it every day. I never thought I'd do it because I'm not the type to sit still and clear my mind. But, clearing your mind and sitting in silence isn't the only way to mediate. When you meditate, ask your angels and guides to guide you. I often say to them, "Please help me figure this out" because I've found that they will not "tell" me anything, but they will help me figure it out.

Initially, I used an app on my iPhone called *Meditation Oasis* created by Mary and Richard Maddux, they also have podcasts on YouTube for meditation. The great thing about this app is that it is *guided*. My mind follows her voice. I don't sit in silence, trying to keep my mind clear. I focus on doing what she says. She has a very calming voice.

I then graduated to *Yoga Nidra* by Kamini Desai, a guided meditation as well, on both iPhone and Android. With *Yoga Nidra* I discovered that there were words that triggered me and this put me on the path of investigating programming. And I began to wonder—why at age 40 was I suddenly claustrophobic? Was it because of programming? So, I really worked at dissolving that program or that trigger.

One way I meditate is with crystals and a copper pyramid that I made myself via instructions from the web. You can find instructions for making your own portable copper pyramid on the "Making Your Own Copper Pyramid" page at the back of this book, online, or you can purchase a copper pyramid online. There are many choices.

Chapter 14
Pyramids

The triangle is an important symbol for me. I remember telling Bob, probably in 2004, that whenever I looked into the sky, all I saw was triangles.

I then read an article about how plants grown in pyramids are healthier. Do a search for yourself, it is terribly fascinating. There are also articles on how you can get a healing under a pyramid. Being that I was into healing, I decided to look for instructions to build my own portable copper pyramid and I found some instructions and built one (Bob did it, but you know what I mean). The parts are simple—four copper pipes from a hardware store, speaker wire, and a split ring.

At first, with the pyramid, I started just sitting in there, then, as an experiment, I put water and left it over night to see if it tasted any different. Pyramid water is supposed to rejuvenate the skin, speed up healing processes, strengthen the immune system, etc. I didn't notice anything at the time, but... that doesn't mean it wasn't changed. Later, I had the idea to meditate in it.

One night, after having my pyramid up for a while, I was showering (after a night of dancing) and felt the menacing feeling of something very negative, be it remote viewers, ETs, or other negative entities, in my shower. There were so many of them. They chased me through my house and into my pyramid (my pyramid is in my spare room). In desperation, I asked my spirit guides what I should do and they showed me a picture in my head of my fingers placed in a triangle shape over my third eye (third chakra). I did that and the room cleared of the negative energy immediately.

Chapter 15
Clearing a Room

Clearing a room is very important. It doesn't seem to help with remote viewers or abductors, but it does clear it of other negative entities and by that I mean anything that feels negative. You can search this information out on the web as well. Clearing is important because negative energy/entities can have an adverse effect on your mood and how you feel about yourself. Have you ever walked into a room and felt like you should run out? That's negative energy. There are energy suckers and energy vampires—even humans who drain you of your precious positive energy. I know people like this and I do protect myself.

Lyn Buchanan wrote a book on remote viewing called *The Seventh Sense: The Secrets of Remote Viewing as told by a "Psychic Spy" for the U.S. Military* and in his book, at the back, are exercises you can do to feel the energy of a room. Some rooms will feel heavy, or cold, or if they don't feel good, then, you need to clear it. There are many ways of clearing a room.

I know you've all heard of "smudging" a room or "clearing" a room with sage. There are smudge sticks you can buy. You can buy sage energy sprays, or incense or other scents you like for clearing a room. You can also use holy water. I tried them all but found I prefer metal Tibetan singing bowls because I have asthma and after a while I noticed a particular sensitivity to smells. So, no scented sprays or incense for me. I use the singing bowl in all rooms of my house including my pyramid. You can bang on them or make them sing by rubbing your striker around the rim. You can buy bowls online at Amazon. They come with a little pillow too. There are crystal singing bowls and metal singing bowls. They come in all sizes and all musical notes.

Crystal skulls protect us from electromagnetic energy coming out of our computer screens and they will heal us. I don't know if you've ever experienced this but I started noticing that whenever I wanted to write something, I'd have all of these great ideas until I got to the computer screen. Then I felt blocked. What if something IS blocking you or affecting you in a negative way from a screen?

I use a variety of skulls: fluorite, geode, rose quartz, etc. I buy a lot of them on Etsy. If you search geode skulls, and get a 3-4 inch one (Geode skulls aren't that expensive), put them around your computer screen. Before using them or any crystal, you should clear them by putting them in a salt bath or using selenite which clears everything. Just place the skull on the selenite and it will do the job.

After a while, or maybe right away, you might hear them talk to you and tell you their name.

I never felt the pull to skulls until a friend took me to a talk about skulls and the person giving the talk spoke of the famous Mitchell-Hedges crystal skull. The speaker had us all in a circle with an inside circle of skulls. I felt nothing, until the end of the speech when two skulls started talking to me. They were telling me that I needed to purchase them and take them home. At first I thought it was unclear just which two skulls were talking. So, I asked them, "Which one of you wants to go home with me?" One of them, a titanium one said, "Me!" and since I knew there were two that initially got my attention, I pointed to another and said, "You?" I didn't get an answer but the rose quartz skull said, "Me." So, I picked that one up and bought them. I meditated with them that night. I guess I needed them at that time. Synchronicity.

After I meditated with the skulls, they told me their names and asked to be placed in certain areas of my room. When my father was ill, I took them with me to California and with the skulls' guidance, put them around his room in a specific configuration. My father was in hospice, but he did get better for a while. Was it the skulls? Or did they help him make a better/easier transition? Unclear. Did it hurt him? No. When I meditated with them, I received healing. The skulls told me to place them near my computer screen—I have a monitor on a stand and I placed the skulls in front to mitigate the negativity coming from the monitor. If you get headaches from staring at your screen/monitor, try putting a few crystal skulls around or in front of your monitor/screen. See if you feel better. What have you got to lose?

Chapter 16
Rocks and Crystals

Because my medium had crystals and rocks all over her office, I became acquainted with the powers of rocks. I am also a rockhound and have been all of my life to Bob's great dismay. Any crystal you are attracted to—is the one for you. For me, Herkimer crystals are very powerful. The clear Herkimer crystals are called "Herkimer diamonds," but the opaque ones are stunning and a very powerful crystal as well.

I use crystals and rocks inside my pyramid to help me meditate and ground. What I'm using right now for my work with abductors are smoky quartz, clear quartz and Herkimer crystals.

Smoky quartz grounds you. Crystal quartz is considered the master of all healing crystal because it amplifies the healing vibrations of other crystals. It also clears the mind of negativity. Herkimer diamonds provide healing and balancing energy. It opens channels for spiritual energy to flow and it opens the crown chakra and third eye chakra.

When I need to change what I'm using, I will hear my spirit guides telling me to purchase other rocks. As with all of the stones I purchase, my guides lead me to certain stones, because they know what I need at that particular time. I purchased Moldavite (a meteorite) because my guides made me feel compelled to search for it online. For a while, I could not get enough of Moldavite, and even purchased some at the local gem show. Like me, you'll just feel the pull to search a certain crystal or rock on Google. Listen to it. It's what you need in your life at that time.

In the past I've used amethyst because it activates spiritual awareness as well as opens intuition and enhances psychic abilities. I used it for opening up my third eye chakra.

When you purchase crystals or rocks, you must "clear" them of any energies negative or otherwise by using a salt bath or selenite. Most people use a salt bath, but I like to use selenite. To clear rocks, crystal, jewelry items, whatever might have negative energies on it, place the item on selenite for 24 hours and the item is cleared. I have bought selenite everywhere from Etsy to Moab, Utah. In Utah, it is less expensive because selenite is found in Utah. You can purchase wands, flat pieces, logs, or whatever. It all works the same. Do not worry about whether the selenite is smooth or not or in a specific shape. It doesn't matter.

Selenite has a powerful vibration and can open, clear, and activate the crown chakra and is excellent for all types of spiritual work. I also place selenite around the inside of my pyramid.

You can do a search of "quartz properties" or whatever rock interests you to find out what they do for you. Do a search of chakras also to work with your crystals.

An excellent merchant for Herkimer quartz crystals is www.rockominerals.com. I've bought his reasonably priced rocks at the Tucson Gem & Mineral Show (that runs for two weeks each February), as well as the Minerology Society of Arizona—they have rock/specimen shows where you can find excellent stones: www.msaaz.org. Or anywhere. I would take special care in knowing the measurements of all crystals you purchase online and shop around—know what you're getting. I think finding these rocks in person is superior to purchasing them online. However, I've also found that these rocks will find me. Recently, I was at a copper mine museum and found the most amazing smoky quartz and it was very inexpensive, less than $15.

Chapter 17
Clues

You might be thinking—there are so many unknowns in my abductions. But, this is not true. You do know a lot, even if it doesn't seem like it.

Look at what you do know. How do you feel when you wake up from an abduction?

I realized early on that whenever I was taken, my clothes smelled. I also noticed that when I came back, I felt hot.

Looking back at that, I was able to distinguish between people and ETs abducting me. I discovered when people took me, I didn't feel hot.

Before the abduction there were clues too. For one thing, I would always feel a sting or something like a mosquito bite and then drop off to sleep. I eventually figured out that this was a mechanism to abduction. I scoured the web for websites on aliens and I found www.Hybridsrising.com and www.Alienjigsaw.com. Both of these sites have information on the types of ETs reported and the tools they use on us. They even had the tools the ETs use for making us sleep. **These are your clues**.

Next, I started really looking at my body and noticed bumps with holes in them, bruises, and other bumps. There were bumps that looked like I had a stun gun used on me. Those were two dots, parallel to each other and sometimes close, sometimes not. I discovered that instead of seeing a square as is sometimes reported—I was really seeing two stun gun marks. Especially on my chest. For some reason, these stun gun marks appear on my chest, back, arms.

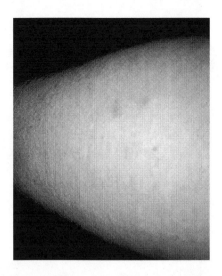

Then, I really started looking at the bruises. The bruises were in patterns. Sometimes three finger marks. Other times, a bruise with a circle in the middle maybe indicating a syringe mark. Other times two circular vertical bruises. It did take me a while to distinguish just what I was looking at.

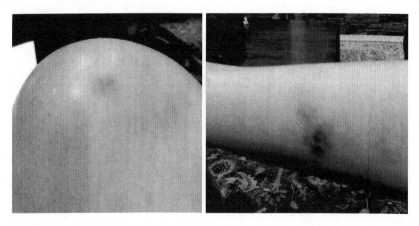

Later, I looked at the bumps on my face. Each morning, near my eyes, there would be at least one large bump with a hole in the middle. This is a syringe mark. Syringe marks are very hard to photograph, but they don't itch and are raised.

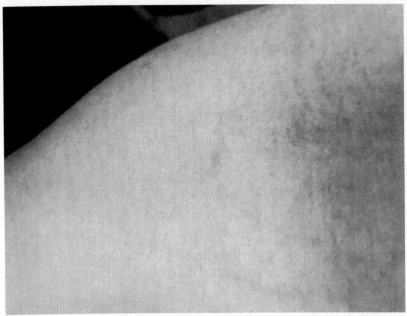
Here is a picture of my arm with a syringe mark. Not much to look at.

I now know that abductors are coming because I get cold and cover myself up with the covers. Most of the time, only my head is showing and this is where the bumps on my face are, which is where they can get to me. These bumps do not itch. They are just raised.

One of the things I really wondered early on was, why would ETs need to use a syringe? The syringe marks solidified my thinking that humans are actually the culprits. It seems the only logical explanation is that I get taken by an ET group and then military at some other time the same night. In the mornings I wake up with my teeth on my left side only feeling like I ate something—but I had just gone to bed after brushing my teeth. In *MILABS* by Dr. Helmut Lammer and Marion Lammer—it says that the military makes you drink something. I have had "dreams" about eating something and drinking something. The obvious questions is: are ETs involved at all? Is this human only?

Early on in 2017 I realized that every month, like clockwork, low-flying airplanes or helicopters showed up wherever I was, home or not. This happened every 6th or 7th of the month. Remember the one dream I had with the neon orange workout top I mentioned earlier? I was wearing that top on one of the nights after a low-flying airplane passed overhead. I obsessively paid attention to all low-flying airplanes after I noticed that they had a pattern. **This is so important. Watch for patterns!** The pattern here is the dates that these planes went over. I do not have a video of these occurrences. One thing that happens is that (1) either they are going over my house late at night when I'm in bed and/or naked (TMI) or (2) if I hear something like a low-flying plane go over my house during the day and I go out to see it, I can't see anything. This means to me (1) either the "plane" is cloaked or (2) the "ship" is not a plane at all and they are using the plane sound to blend in.

Telepathy is real. Don't think that the military hasn't figured this out. I regularly block them from my mind. You should do the same. You need to say, "**My mind is CLOSED**" silently. You should say this silently to yourself whenever you feel vulnerable. Anytime you hear conversations in your head that involve you. Sometimes, I'll have beings/people interfere/intrude in my thoughts. One thing I've noticed is that when I say, "my mind is closed," I can still hear THEIR conversations to each other in my head but they will say, "She blocked us, Sir." Or something to that effect. This is one of the things I've used in a trial and error approach to telepathy intrusion. I didn't invite them into my head. It is an intrusion.

When planes/vehicles go over my house—I hear tones in my ears start up.

I think the remote viewers check back to see if I'm asleep all night long and I leave my bed and am brought back sometime later.

I have found that if I am given the shot to sleep and I don't sleep right away, I will stay awake for hours. They will keep coming back to try to shoot me up with sleeping stuff. If I resist, I stay awake for another few hours until I can no longer stay awake.

Write down your dreams as soon as you can. Dreams are like smoke and they disappear quickly.

Use **LaHoChi** each morning and eventually work up to every night and every morning. If you don't build up your frequency, you will be awake all night. Heal yourself after an abduction but if you use **LaHoChi** at night before an abduction, it can wire you like caffeine can. Don't use LaHoChi at night before abduction until you have done it every day for a month.

CHAPTER 18

DREAMS

I have been keeping a dream journal for the last three years, and I've learned a few things I want to share with you.

I think all dreams are remote views or memories. When we have blank spots, that's when our memories are removed.

I started noticing, probably in my 20s, that when I dreamed, I couldn't read anything or hear anyone talk on the phone. The writing was scribbled and if I was trying to talk on a phone, I couldn't hear anything and that meant, it was a dream and I would wake up.

Remote viewing is a skill and some remote viewers can read in their views. I just started being able to read in my dreams about 10 years ago. But, I didn't write any of those dreams of 10 years ago down, not understanding the significance. When I intentionally remote view (while I'm awake), I can sometimes read words, name tags, book titles, etc. About two years ago, I had a dream where I was on the phone and I heard someone talking on the other end of the line. This was my first experience of hearing someone talk back to me on the phone in a dream. It was the FBI telling me they wanted to interview me. It was exciting! It showed me that I had changed and I could now hear and read in my dreams. Progress.

There are theories out there that indicate that "you" are everything in your dreams or that dreams are symbols and a symbol dictionary is provided to help you. I do not believe any of those theories. Instead, it is my belief that dreams are either memories of what really happened or screen memories that mask what really happened with what your mind can handle. Whitley Strieber's book, *Communion*, touches on the "screen memory" which is the mind's way of protecting you by alleviating trauma. The ETs would like you to think that they are the architect of your dreams/screen memories, but it is your own mind. If you look behind your dreams, using remote view techniques, you can see what is really there. For instance, if I have a dream that I lost my purse and I search everywhere for it and my entire dream is the stress of that experience, this says to me that I was stressed. And this means that something was happening to me that was stressing me out and my mind was working out a way to tell me that I was stressed by giving me a typical experience that shows me that I'm stressed. The truth is that while I was stressed, my mind gave me a screen memory—because my psyche can handle losing my purse, but it can't handle the truth of what was really going on behind the screen memory.

Consider this "dream":

9/5/17 Dream – I was with two or three army guys on another planet looking for rocks. We dug a big hole making a mound of dirt and we were sifting through the dirt from the mound we made. It was dark. One of the army men thought something bit him in his boot and struggled to get it off. He started yelling and frantically untying it. He had extremely long shoelaces and had tied it around his boot several times between the heel and ball and up his green ski pants. When he finally got his boot off there was nothing there. He added rocks and sand to his boot to try to get the bug creature out of it. He gave an explanation of why he was doing that but although I tried to repeat it, it didn't make sense and I couldn't remember it (even in the dream).

While digging on the mound I found something. One of the soldiers took credit for finding it and said it was the thing we were looking for. Then he ran off to activate it. In the meantime, I saw all of these beautiful stones and began picking them up and showing them to another soldier. They were beauts. Some were circular crystals, like barrels of crystal. I was lying down while digging. Suddenly, I found this curious square slab of rock. It was the size of my palm. I touched it and it activated, then a big shadow appeared. The army guy came back and said to the other soldier that the rock was not right but this one, the one I found—was the one they were looking for—again taking credit for finding it.

A cat, or some other animal, started fishing in the water and bringing us rocks with pointy teeth on them. These rocks were pink and the teeth were white. After bringing about 10 of these small pink rocks with pointy teeth, a big rock came out and this one looked like the mouth of a beast! Finally the cat coaxed out a big water animal that looked like a sting ray. The sting ray came to me and one of the soldiers called out, "We found the sting ray!" but it was too loud there for anyone to hear.

This above "dream" is to me, a memory of something that I actually did. It is strange and it is specific. Why would any army personnel need me to activate anything? Consider your own dreams. What could they tell you about your life when you sleep?

Chapter 19
Abductors are MIMICS

Over the two years of going to her, my medium spoke to me at length about knowing how everything FELT in my heart as opposed to seeing something. I wanted to SEE so that I could understand what was going on in my life with the ETs. I felt by SEEING I could judge the situation. I could see their body language, their facial expressions, etc., as I do when I read people or situations now. At the time, I felt seeing was most important. If I couldn't SEE, I could not understand.

Because I could not SEE the ETs, she wanted me to FEEL how they FELT so that I would know intuitively if they were good and trustworthy. If they felt like LOVE, I could speak with them, converse, learn, etc. However, I could never feel anything when faced with the ETs. I could only feel neutrality or negativity.

My medium was wrong. ETs can mimic human emotions, and so, it is a fallacy that we should as humans strive to "feel" how an ET feels. ETs don't feel and they are negative, for the most part, at least those who are taking us are. To feel is not the right course of action. The correct way to determine an entity's (human or ET) trustworthiness is from our soul. Our soul can tell us if this person/ET is someone or something we should or can associate with without fail. If anyone is telling you, medium or not, that you are a failure because you cannot feel the LOVE from an ET, they are wrong. You are not a failure. It is not possible because ETs mimic human emotions to trick us into trusting them. The trap is trusting their faked emotions and feeling the love they are sending to us to keep us feeling their goodness so we think the abductions are for altruism.

Chapter 20
Fear

I don't want you to think that I am never scared. I used to be scared every night and I'm still scared now, but I know I will remember something that will help me. However, there are nights that I feel menaced and this means that I feel a horrible negativity has entered my room, and there is a presence or many presences of negativity and heaviness in my room.

Everyone knows what it's like to get the "willies" or the "heebie-jeebies." This is what it feels like, but a lot of times, the fear is overwhelming. It makes it hard to sleep, that's for sure. And you know that when you finally sleep that night, that something horrible is going to happen, so you try to stay awake as long as possible. You try anything and everything. Eventually, you succumb. It is a helpless and horrible feeling.

These days, I'm still scared. But, I'm furious and I know I can use any information that I remember or have as a screen memory against them by using remote viewing. I suggest either taking a remote viewing course like the one offered by David Morehouse or reading Stewart A. Swerdlow's book: *The Hyperspace Helper A User-Friendly Guide* and specifically using *the Green Spiral Staircase* exercise. In some ways, I don't feel as hopeless as I used to but I also know that I am using whatever I can against them and it feels good. I have leveled the playing field. You can too. There is hope.

One thing I want to say about fear—this is how they control us. It's what keeps us silent. What would happen if we all started talking about this issue and confirming each other's stories, and compared notes? That will not help them, but it will help us.

Chapter 21
Implant in Eyeball

On **9/14/17** I wrote this about my eye implant:

"I have discovered that LaHoChi will dissolve knots in my body by asking the LaHoChi master to dissolve it. After finding this healing technique, my eye implant went crazy and instead of being a round light, it changed shapes and vibrated. Which looks kind of like a blob with a tail."

I have an implant in both eyes, but the one in my right eye is much more active. It's a bright white light. I see it rebooting and turning on at various times during the day and night. It looks like that round spot that you see when you rub your eye, but it turns on every night and it is very bright. I turn it off at night by turning my head to the right quickly over and over. It always comes back on, but I hate that feeling of being watched, so I either close my eyes or I turn it off over and over. During the day it turns on and I think whoever put it in there is watching me or recording me through my own eyes. I have been to the ophthalmologist and go every four months because as a disclaimer, I do have glaucoma in my right eye (damaged optical nerve) from eye surgery done in 2015. However, even when I do go to the ophthalmologist and tell him about these lights, he doesn't see anything. To him, everything is "normal."

While typing this book I saw a floater going down the page in my peripheral vision independently, line by line. I had to unplug from the internet, save this book locally and then use a tool from *Healing Archetypes & Symbols* by Stewart A. Swerdlow and Janet Diane Mourglia-Swerdlow, called "Cancellation" to cancel whatever was watching me via my eyes. The outline for using these tools is located at the back of the book. I do not know what or who put the implant in my eye . I have not been able to cancel it or get rid of it in any way. Or, if I do feel like I've been successful in cancelling it, it goes away for a time and then someone puts it or another one back in. These implants look different. Some are very bright and some are striped. Yes, I can see the implant. It's in the corner of my right eye and while in bed, at night, if I look over, I can see a bright light in the corner. The light in the left eye is also in the corner but is not as bright. These lights drive me bonkers and I feel very used by them. Who is looking through my eyes? To see what? For what purpose? I don't have the answers but it's important for me to share with you what is possible.

I used to have these spiny black things I saw in my eye and went to the ophthalmologist about and I never thought about them again until one day about a month ago I saw one and my knee jerk reaction to anything unusual is: **cancellation**. It disappeared.

I have seen a brown barrier in my left eye in the peripheral vision and cancelled it (7/16/19) but then saw flickering. I could not cancel out the white flickering. It is still there.

Chapter 22
Teaching/Sharing These Tools with Others

My first attempt at teaching this material was with people I met at a meditation group in January 2019. I was so excited after finding these tools that I invited them to my house to share them and talk about them. I showed them the material and tried to show them how they could use the tools in their daily lives. This did not work out at all. These people did not see the value in these tools and, worse, since they felt they were *not* being abducted, the material was meaningless. Being abducted is a lonely, isolated existence, and even though these people did not judge me or ridicule me, they also did not see the importance of such tools. They didn't use them. Clearly, I was wasting my time and breath. I had two meetings and gave up on this group.

Chapter 24
Searching for Help

Over time, I learned that I needed to find something else to help me with the ETs. Psychics and mediums could not help me with being abducted. I felt hopeless, depressed and I couldn't talk to anyone about this. I asked my guides for help.

In 2017 I took a healing class called LaHoChi by Elizabeth Patric and also, Integrated Energy Therapy (IET) by Stevan J. Thayer, aka angelic healing. My medium taught both. Being a type-A personality of sorts, I wanted to learn all about healing. I wanted to take all of the classes and learn everything I could. I saw some books at Amazon called *The Healers Handbook* and *Healing Archetypes and Symbols by Stewart A. Swerdlow and Janet Diane Mourglia-Swerdlow.* I bought them. At the time, these books were waaaaayyyyy over my head. I put them aside.

My medium believed that I made soul contracts for abduction, which are agreements we make with other souls before we are born. Other souls we have contracts with will be those that will bring deep changes into our lives through unique circumstances. These contracts are to teach us important lessons we've chosen to learn before reincarnation. So, this means, that it was her belief that we and everyone chose our lives and our abduction contracts. Because of these contracts, she believed that she could help me break the abduction contracts and although we tried everything she knew, we could not stop the abductions by trying to break contracts.

After trying unsuccessfully to break contracts with ETs, I asked my guides for help again. They guided me back to the Swerdlows' books. This was Thanksgiving 2018.

I was going on vacation to Mexico at the time and my guides made me feel that I better bring those books with me, so I did. They told me after I cracked them open that it was because I needed to get out of my environment (with phones/TVs, life) in order to have the time, energy, etc. to look at these books with new eyes.

I realized that my manifesto of sacred space and protections wasn't working. Whatever I was trying to keep out was walking through. It didn't matter if I stated my sovereignty or declared my right to free will. I stopped using all setting space and protections each night.

In January 2019, I stopped going to the medium.

With great excitement and input from my spirit guides, I decided to show my medium my outline of what I'd learned from these books. I brought the books and the outline with me to one of our sessions. The sight of the book cover caused her to make a face and stick her tongue out to show her distaste. She was against these tools. She must have thought I was asking for her "blessing" to use these tools. I wasn't. I was sharing them with her as my spirit guides asked me to show her, as I am with you, and telling her we could collaborate and help other abductees that she ran across. But, no. These tools were not her "teachings." So, we parted ways. She taught me a lot about angels, guides, crystals, etc., but my guides told me that whatever she saw and told me, the abductors also knew because her knowing was like a broadcast. I decided to become my own mentor. As you can imagine, the remote viewers really stepped up their game after that.

Not having the slightest idea where to go from there, I had the bright idea in February 2019, to contact the only organization I know that deals with UFOs and hopefully people like me. So, I went to the Mutual UFO Network (MUFON) website, answered questions on their questionnaire and received a call from a member of their MUFON Experiencer Research Team (ERT). I told her my "encounter" stories, two of the few times I have seen them with my own eyes and she mentioned someone in a meetup group that did UFO talks that I might be able to connect with. I contacted that person and met with him. I bought him a set of the two Swerdlow books I had been working with, and gave him a little tutorial on what I was talking about. He said he would allow me some time in his group to give a little 15-20 minute talk. I was scheduled to give a talk about these tools on March 23, 2019 with his UFO group. My father became sick on March 20, 2019 and I had to postpone. On May 25, 2019, I met with the ERT member and brought the books with me, gave her a set and gave her the same spiel/tutorial that I gave the UFO meetup guy. She told me to write this book. I was hesitant. A book? Me? I gave my talk on June 29, 2019 in that meetup group and the ERT member came to support me. I hate public speaking, but this is important, so I did it.

On, August 4, 2019 I was at an experiencer support group meeting (information in resources section on page 211) and heard about Terry Lovelace, who wrote a book called *Incident at Devil's Den, a True Story*. I bought Terry's book that same day and when I received it, I read it in one sitting. First, to learn anything about his experience, and second, he was one of my people! I then wrote a review on Amazon and challenged myself and others to write about their experiences so that we can talk about this and stop hiding. Make this topic mainstream!

CHAPTER 25

KNOWING YOU ARE ON THE RIGHT TRACK

By happenstance I went to an angelic message night around December 2018, and my message was that I was leveling the playing field. I had not told anyone that I was using these marvelous tools. As far as I was concerned it was an experiment. I could feel the difference but what if it was my imagination? But it wasn't. **I was making progress.** Each night, I would be abducted, the next day I would write in my notebook and write down everything I remembered, all dreams, I would smell my clothes. If my clothes smelled, I would know I left. If they didn't, I would know I stayed home. I kept a notebook—a journal—that listed everything that happened to me with all of my "adventures," what I figured out, then I remote viewed my dreams and saw and wrote that down. I wrote down anything that could be considered important data of any kind.

After a while (approximately two months), I noticed that it felt like it was quieter, fewer abductions, then I started being able to tell that there were different groups, each taking their turns abducting me. There were the Draco's (which are a reptilian type of being), the Mantis, the Grays. There were military people who came to take me to a mine on certain nights. There were humans who took me in the helicopters on the 6th or 7th of the month. After spending a lot of time doing remote viewing and using the tools I found in the Swerdlow's books: *Healing Archetypes & Symbols* and *The Hyperspace Helper: A User-Friendly Guide*, I was able to piece together, over time, what was really going on. As you can see by my journal entries, this figuring out really started accelerating when I found the above Swerdlow books and was able to use *The Green Spiral Staircase* exercise, and ALL of the other exercises in the *Hyperspace Helper* to illuminate what was happening when I was away from my bed. Each night, I would take notes, so to speak. I would notice what I saw, felt, heard, and would methodically write down each and every clue the next day and then I would methodically do the same each and every night until I had a better picture. When I did see whatever horrible scene I saw, I would use the tools: specifically **Cancellation** from the *Healing Archetypes* book to cancel out those things/entities/scenarios, etc., that I did not want in my life anymore. Using these tools, Cancellation, a protector tool (called Ultimate Protection) and remote viewing via the Green Spiral Staircase exercise plus others in the *Hyperspace Helper* book, I was able to delete multiple people, entities, etc., from my life.

CHAPTER 26
THE TOOLS AKA
THE BIG GUNS

Overview

Disclaimer: You will be punished by the abductors for using these tools. For writing this book and telling all I know, the abductors punished me regularly. This means: pain in the left side of my head, left shoulder, left arm, and eye problems. I have also had itchy skin. And because of memory wipes, I have no idea the extent of my "punishment."

This is dangerous stuff. They will erase your memory, but you will suffer before the memory wipe. Proceed at your own risk.

1. Buy these two books in paperback (I found mine at Amazon):
    a. *Healing Archetypes & Symbols* by Stewart A. Swerdlow and Janet Diane Mourglia-Swerdlow.
    b. *The Hyperspace Helper: A User-Friendly Guide* by Stewart A. Swerdlow and Janet D. Swerdlow

Paperbacks are useful for dog-earing pages and going back and forth. If you can do this on Kindle, more power to you. But, you will need both books at the same time during exercises, at least at first.

2. **LaHoChi – Energy Self-Healing**. Go to www.lahochi.com and buy the attunement **(you must have the attunement to be able to heal yourself)** and the book. The whole package will cost you under $100. **This is SO important**. Set up your appointment with **Elizabeth Patric** to obtain your attunement, which is done remotely. You will just go to bed and receive it.

Read through the four hand positions for self-healing and **memorize** them. You can heal yourself after each and every abduction and anytime in between. If, after abduction, you can't sleep, **LaHoChi self-healing will help**. I do this and it REALLY helps. I do not get a kickback or anything for mentioning this page. This energy healing modality just really helps me, more than any other and it will help you too.

3. **Meditation.** Use any guided meditation that speaks to you. I used *Meditation Oasis* at first because I could not sit still. I could not remove my thoughts. These meditations are guided. *Meditation Oasis* is not on Android as of this writing, but *Yoga Nidra* is on both platforms—another good one. **Meditate daily if possible. Meditation fights back against abductors because it gets around programming** and speaks to your SOUL. The abductors cannot stop this. They can't know what you know and what you've been told by your soul unless YOU tell them. Don't tell them!

Meditation is a cornerstone and a must-have with these tools. You must use both meditation and LaHoChi for healing and these tools, to get the best results. LaHoChi and meditation are the foundation of the healing tools. Meditation allows for information to get through to you via your SOUL and it's a way for you to heal.

Keep a notebook handy for any great ideas/thoughts you may have while meditating. You can also go to meditation groups. Meditate for healing, comfort, relaxation, when you feel overwhelmed, scared, etc. You could even create a pyramid, like me, to meditate in. **If you feel stuck, go back to meditation. Being stuck means you haven't meditated in a while.**

4. Confirmation Signal: You must obtain a confirmation signal with your oversoul or higher self during meditation. You get this confirmation signal by meditating and asking your oversoul or higher self for it.

5. Ultimate Protection Affirmation: Protection is required for using any tools in the books. On page 67-68 of *Healing Archetypes & Symbols* by Steward A. Swerdlow and Janet Diane Mourglia-Swerdlow, you will see the Ultimate Protection tool.

Ultimate Protection:
"I am always protected. I am always protected wherever I go and whatever I do."

Make sure you read both pages. **Silently**, say this affirmation to yourself. You need to place yourself in a violet (not purple) tetrahedron and a violet (not purple) octahedron with a golden sphere around the whole thing. When I first read this book, I didn't see that last part and missed octahedron. You need it.

When you are doing this work, because you will be a detective of your own life, **you need protection**. **The ETs will punish you for this work and doing these things**. I'm just warning you.

6. **Golden Triangle**: As an added layer of protection, I always add a **golden triangle** over the whole Ultimate Protection. I started doing that because after using the **Ultimate Protection**, I found I needed something more because the **Ultimate Protection** lasted only 2 days for me. A **golden triangle** helps. This is just something I have learned through trial and error.

7. Using *Healing Archetypes & Symbols* by Stewart A. Swerdlow and Janet Diane Mourglia-Swerdlow, on page 28 there is an affirmation called Cancellation. It reads as follows:

   Cancellation:
   I now "brown x" out all unnecessary negativity in my life. I now "brown x" out all <u>*fill in the blank*</u> according to the wishes of my oversoul and god-mind."

   (Important! Say both sentences silently each time in your mind. Otherwise it doesn't work.)

   I like words, but you can also visualize a brown x. I memorized this affirmation and used it for anything and everything. For example: diabetes in my family, sugar cravings, weight gain, fear of math, injustice, bullies, psychic attack, narcissists, you name it. Why not? I'm eliminating **unnecessary negativity**, in whatever form that takes. I write this all down and see if it goes away. I do methodical experiments. I write everything down.

a. **Signal from Oversoul:** It is imperative that you know if the cancellation worked. You need a signal from your oversoul that is definitely **yes** and definitely **no**. You should also know if your oversoul is signaling that you didn't quite make the mark.

b. **Readers:** Go meditate now and ask your guides/oversoul or higher self for that signal. It can be a green check mark, a fart, hiccup, itchy nose, etc. Don't tell anyone what your signal is. If the ETs/military abductors know, then they'll block it.

c. **Qualifiers**: I found that I sometimes needed qualifiers to use **cancellation** most effectively because what I was trying to remove was too broad. By that I mean:

   All remote viewers in this house, all AI (artificial intelligence) on my computer, all military personnel, all Grays in my room, all Mantis, anything I saw in my dreams, any vehicles in all dimensions. I have found that [all dimensions] is an important one.

d. **Be specific.** Sometimes I use them all at once. It can be cumbersome, but your signal will tell you if you **almost** cancelled it out and if you didn't. If you can't **cancel it** out, you might need more or fewer qualifiers, you might want to try a different way of describing it altogether or it might be something you have to live with—for now.

e. **Never say any of these affirmations out loud.** They are listening! ETs and military abductors are narcissists! Narcissists listen to you and use everything you say against you for their own agenda.

f. **Write everything down that you cancel out and if you can or can't cancel it.** This is an important habit to get into. Some examples: "I now brown x out all unnecessary negativity in my life, I now brown x out all programming, in all dimensions that is causing me to cough right now." Did you stop coughing? What signal did you receive from your oversoul to indicate that you were successful? If you were unsuccessful, then try other wording. "I now brown x out all unnecessary negativity in my life. I now brown x out anyone or anything in all dimensions causing me to cough right now." Did that work? Did you get the signal? This is all trial and error for your particular situation. What diseases do you have? What entities do you have in your life? This is why I use qualifiers because you need them to make granular cancellations.

The **cancellation tool** is not a once a day affirmation. It should be called a **mantra**. Whenever you see something that is negative, cancel it out. ETs, ghosts, remote viewers, etc. **Get used to saying it.** Memorize it so that you can use it when you need it, in the middle of the night or just waking up, or whenever. **It should be a kneejerk reaction to negativity**. Use it always.

An important note: These affirmations work because we are not asking someone else to choose our highest and best good. Some might say to you: "Ask for whatever is in your highest and best good, best and highest healing, best interests." **This is a loophole**. **Ask who? Who decides** what is in your highest and best good? In asking for "highest good" we are giving our power away to someone else. Are we supposed to HOPE that the entity is nice and decides in our favor? In using **cancellation,** we are asking our higher self/oversoul and god-mind to decide what is best for us. And that is the way it should be.

NEXT, **REMOTE VIEW** USING THE FOLLOWING BOOK:

8. *The Hyperspace Helper: A User-Friendly Guide,* by Stewart A. Swerdlow and Janet D. Swerdlow. If I have a dream or a blank spot, I use this book to explore it. A very helpful exercise is *the Green Spiral Staircase*. This is essentially a way to remote view. You can go back to your screen memories and look at what's really happening and then, you guessed it, cancel out what is negative. Follow what the book tells you and don't pressure yourself to see anything. This is a tool to help you get to the bottom of what is really happening. Be creative. The Green Spiral Staircase instructions are below:

Green Spiral Staircase Visualization: "The *Green Spiral Staircase* visualization is an investigative procedures designed to mentally time-travel to specific events in your existence that are blocked from reaching your conscious mind...

Preliminaries: Take two or three cleansing breaths. Center your consciousness in royal blue at the pineal gland (third eye area). Put a royal blue circle with a royal blue dot in the middle at your pineal gland. Put the rest of your body in medium green to activate the memory centers of the brain. Use a visual aid if necessary.

Visualize a green spiral staircase in front of you in the same medium green in which your body is now.

Focus on a specific event, time period, or place that you need to remember in detail.

Start descending the staircase while holding this thought in mind.

At some point, you will feel a need or urge to step off the staircase. This signifies that you have reached the layer in your subconscious mind that holds the memory.

Step off the staircase

Observe whatever scenes are in front of you as if they were on a television set or in a movie. <u>Do not</u> participate in them.

If you become upset or traumatized to the point that you no longer wish to continue, immediately place yourself completely in brown. Discontinue the exercise.

If you see a scene and wonder if it is true, a product of your imagination, or even a hallucination, place the scene in pale orange. Pale orange is the color of absolute truth. A true scene stays in pale orange. If not, you will see the color change.

Continue to observe the scenes in front of you for as long as you wish.

When you have seen enough or, if the scene ends, go back up to the staircase to the place where you began and stop.

Do not go beyond this place. Step off the staircase.

Place yourself in brown.

View your royal blue circle with the royal blue dot in your pineal gland.

Write down your observations.

Your mind will show you only the pertinent information that you currently need to know, not a minute by minute description.

Be patient and do not give up on seeing behind your screen memories. If you repeatedly can't see anything, be creative. Mentally devise methods that allow you to break through the memory barriers. For example, you might create a violet saw to cut through the walls or an illumination tool. This is your own mind. You can invent anything you need at any moment.

Being consistent and persistent are both extremely important."

ONE LAST IMPORTANT AND USEFUL TOOL:

9. **Yahweh**. **Yahweh** is a form of the Hebrew name of God used in the Bible. You also sometimes see it a Yahveh or YHWH. The definition is God and it is used especially by the ancient Hebrews. This is a very powerful word. ETs all scatter when this word is used. You can also use soul sounds. If you hear other sounds while you're using Yahweh, like TU or TEE or NO, or whatever, say them. These sounds are individual to you, to your soul.

One night, I woke up and realized both eyes were blurry. I put drops in. I have a fragile right eye and I keep drops on the bedside table. I put in artificial tears and…. nothing, still blurry. I freaked out. I was pacing around my room and then the den. Suddenly, a thought pops into my head. **Yahweh**. I have nothing to lose so I start saying: Yaaaaaahhhhhhweeeeeeehhhhhh, kind of singing it. My eyes cleared up. I could see again.

After that night, I use this word **Yahweh** all the time. I can feel the ETs leaving. They are afraid of this word. I know this because I take notes of everything. Be methodical and write everything down for your experiments. This way, you'll know when you're making progress.

You will also need the following:

1. **Persistence.** Become a detective of your nighttime life. Investigate the hell out of it. Know who, what, and where. Write it all down and look back and **cancel**!
2. A notebook for writing down dreams, thoughts, any messages received in meditation. If you type anything up, they will know everything you're doing. They are on our computers.
3. **A pack of colored pens (I use gel).** I see a lot of things in my dreams/memories/remote views that I usually want to draw. A lot of them are in color, so I attempt to draw them and color them. A lot of times this helps me remember the dream.

4. **The things you will see will not make sense and will be disjointed**. Do not let this discourage you. They are just pieces of the puzzle of your abductions and life.

Chapter 27
What I do, Step by Step

When I first found these books, I had to work with them using trial and error. You will find this out too. Trial and error is the only way, I think, to really figure these puzzles out, because that's what they are. In the way that people can be puzzles, so can the workings of the abduction by either ET or military, there could be numerous groups of ETs and endless covert military programs. The military entities I have seen do not have emblems that I recognize but we are all different and abducted for different reasons. We all have different experiences, lives, etc. I don't know that your experiences are my experiences, but hopefully you can see what has worked for me and use the similarities to blast these buttheads out of our lives.

Sorry if these are a bit repetitive. But, initially, it is necessary to remember these steps.

1. Purchase a spiral notebook and a pen. Keep them together.

2. Purchase the following two books in paperback.

    a. *Healing Archetypes & Symbols* by Stewart A. Swerdlow and Janet Diane Mourglia-Swerdlow.

    b. *The Hyperspace Helper: A User-Friendly Guide* by Stewart A. Swerdlow and Janet D. Swerdlow

3. Purchase the LaHoChi book and attunement from www.lahochi.com. Do this once.

4. Meditate every day, in any way you choose. Get into this habit. This is a healing mechanism.

5. In Meditation:

    a. Ask your oversoul/higher self for a **Yes** and **No** signal. **Memorize it**. Do this once.

b. Ask your "**archangels and support teams of light**" to guide you and help you figure things out. **Do this every time**.

c. Ask **silently**, in your mind. **Never ask these things out loud**. They are listening. They want to know what you're thinking or what you know.

d. Information is power.

e. Information is currency.

6. Set your **ultimate protection** in your mind, **never out loud**, which is:

    a. Seeing yourself in a violet tetrahedron then putting yourself into a violet octahedron.

    b. Add a **golden sphere** around it. If you find that it's not enough protection, add a **golden triangle** over the whole thing.

    c. Say, silently to yourself, "I am always protected. I am always protected wherever I go and whatever I do."

    d. Do this every two or three days. Only you will know if it works for you and if you need the **golden triangle**.

    e. **Never** state your **ultimate protection** out loud. They are listening. They want to know what you're thinking or what you know.

        f. Information is power.

        g. Information is currency.

        h. Write down what works in your notebook.

7. Use Yahweh.

    a. When I first heard of this word, I used it. I used it for everything. At first, it scared the bejeebus out of all ETs.

Later, it did not work as well, because I think, I was dealing with a different layer of ETs, but I still use it occasionally. You have nothing to lose. Use it and if it doesn't work, the below tool will work. Or, use them together!

   b. You can say **Yahweh** silently or out loud.

8. Memorize the cancellation tool: "I now 'brown x' out all unnecessary negativity in my life. I now 'brown x' out all <u>*fill in the blank [in all dimensions]*</u> according to the wishes of my oversoul and god-mind." You will need both sentences for this tool to work.

   a. State this tool silently, in your mind. **Never state the cancellation tool out loud**. They are listening. They want to know what you're thinking or what you know.

   b. Information is power.

   c. Information is currency.

9. State "I now 'brown x' out all unnecessary negativity in my life. I now 'brown x out' all sleep darts in all dimensions or **anything you're facing.**

   a. Write down what you cancel out and if you get the **Yes** or **No** signal.

   b. If you get **No**, try again.

   c. If you get a **Maybe**, add more qualifiers until you get a **Yes.** Which means, if you get a maybe from your oversoul, add or subtract a qualifier. Keep saying things in your head until you get the **Yes**. Keep notes. For example: "I now 'brown x' out all unnecessary negativity in my life. I now 'brown x' out all remote viewers in all dimensions in the room right now." Maybe? Then change it to: "I now 'brown x' out all unnecessary negativity in my life. I now 'brown x' out all remote viewers in all dimensions who made that noise in my room right now." Did you get a yes to that? If so, YAY! If not, keep adding qualifiers to your statement to get rid of the unnecessary negativity.

   d. Don't give up.

   e. **Never add qualifiers out loud.** They are listening. They want to know what you're thinking or what you know.

   f. Information is power.

   g. Information is currency.

10. Write down everything you experience in your notebook.

11. **Trust No One and No Thing.** I can't stress this enough!

12. **Payment.** If any entity wants to help you, you **must ask for an exchange**. That means, you must give them something back. Or, if you can help them, you must get something in exchange. That's how everything works. It's not about money, it's bartering. This is why I say information is currency. It is imperative that you get their agreement before any transaction occurs. I always barter for something I need at that time, like blocking remote viewers or protection or giving me a signal when a particular entity is near. It has to be something that money can't buy. It has to be something they can give. I don't want to be specific in what I ask for because I'm typing this on my computer and if I'm specific they may block it. You do not know who or what these entities are or what they can do. Use caution. Use common sense. Be fearful of them, so that you don't barter anything you can't pay for.

13. If you hear entities talking in your head (telepathy), use the cancellation tool. Never assume anyone talking to you is good.

   a. Write down what you cancel out and if you get the **Yes** or **No** signal.

   b. If you get **No**, try again.

- c. If you get a **Maybe**, add more qualifiers until you get a **Yes**.
- d. Don't give up.
- e. Use **Yahweh** whenever you can.
- f. For telepathy, I have blocked them by saying, "My mind is closed." I also ask my spirit guides to block them.
- g. **Cancel** silently, in your mind. **Never cancel** out loud. They are listening. They want to know what you're thinking or what you know.
- h. Information is power.
- i. Information is currency.
- j. You can also say **"My mind is CLOSED"** to shut them out.

14. If you hear a **snap**, a **crack** or a **thunk**, these sounds are remote viewers **working for the abductors in my experience**. They are watching you and reporting back. The sounds are different for the different types of entities that are remote viewing us. Remote viewers can be neutral, but in our case, that doesn't mean for us. It usually means, **against us**, in my experience.

    - a. Use the **cancellation tool**. Write down what you cancel out and if you get the **Yes** or **No** signal.
    - b. If you get **No**, try again.
    - c. If you get a **Maybe**, add more qualifiers until you get a **Yes**.
    - d. Don't give up.
    - e. Cancel silently, in your mind. **Never cancel out loud**. They are listening. They want to know what you're thinking or what you know.
    - f. Information is power.
    - g. Information is currency.

h. Write down what works and what doesn't work for you. This is about you.

i. Write legibly, in case you need to read it over later.

15. Listen for noises, wherever you are. **Pay attention to your environment**! Notice everything you can.

    a. At work?

    b. At the movies?

        i. If feel tingling at the movies, don't assume it's a good thing. **Cancel** to be sure!

        ii. If you feel pressure in your head, **cancel** it!

    c. At a bar?

    d. Someone else's house?

    e. Outside?

    f. In the shower?

    g. Your house?

        i. FYI. Your house is NOT "settling." If it's windy and your house is making noises, then yes, it's settling. If the noise follows you. It is remote viewers.

        ii. If you feel pressure changes in your house, this is a remote viewer.

        iii. If you hear clicking, tones in your ears, etc., cancel those out too, wherever you are. No matter what. Get in that habit of **cancelling** anything and everything that you are unclear of its purpose or if it's good.

    h. Your car?

      i. The water bottles in your car should not make cracking noises or change in elevation noises. There should be NO cracking, thunking, or snapping of anything in your car. You should not feel tingles in your car. If you do, then, use the **cancellation tool!**

     ii. Write down what you cancel out and if you get the **Yes** or **No** signal.

    iii. If you get **No**, try again.

    iv. If you get a **Maybe**, add more qualifiers until you get a **Yes**.

     v. If your maybe never turns into a **Yes,** write that down and go back to it later.

    vi. Cancel silently, in your mind. **Never cancel out loud**. They are listening. They want to know what you're thinking or what you know.

   vii. Information is power.

  viii. Information is currency.

16. In the shower:

    a. If you hear or feel anything in the shower that is not the norm, use the **cancellation tool. Don't talk to anything or anyone assuming they are to your benefit**. I had to learn this the hard way. Once, while I was showering someone or something started talking to me and I started feeling tingly all over. I thought this was good. It wasn't. My head started hurting and my eyesight got blurry and I suddenly had to call my angels and ask for help and when that didn't work, I had to contact the medium and ask for a healing and for her to see what was going on so that she could fix it. She was able to help me that time, but I learned a valuable lesson. Don't assume anyone or anything that interacts with you is good.

b. Using the **cancelation tool**, wait for the **Yes** or **No** signal.

c. If you get **No**, try again.

d. If you get a **Maybe**, add more qualifiers until you get a **Yes**.

e. Don't give up.

f. Don't freak out.

g. If you hear Morse code like beeping anywhere, **cancel it!**

h. If you feel tingles, **cancel it.** Let your oversoul determine if it's negative or not. Even if you are meditating and expect to feel tingles, cancel it.

i. No matter what you feel or hear in the shower that is not part of your regular routine, **cancel it!** Be safe!

j. **Cancel** silently, in your mind. **Never cancel** out loud. They are listening. They want to know what you're thinking or what you know.

k. Information is power.

l. Information is currency.

m. Write down what happened in your notebook, for future reference.

17. Clicking or tones in your ears?

    a. Use the **cancelation tool**, wait for the **Yes** or **No** signal.

    b. If you get **No**, try again.

    c. If you get a **Maybe**, add more qualifiers until you get a **Yes**.

    d. Don't give up.

e. **Cancel** silently, in your mind. **Never cancel out loud**. They are listening. They want to know what you're thinking or what you know.

   f. Information is power.

   g. Information is currency.

   h. Write down what happened in your notebook, for future reference.

18. Notice the times you get remote viewers and what types:

Are there thunks (humans)?

   a. Snaps (invisible beings)? or

   b. Cracks (ETs)?

   c. What are their habits?

   d. I have talked to them to figure this out. Ask them why they are there. Maybe they'll talk to you too.

At Night!

19. Before bed (any time before bed), **meditate.**

20. Put a notebook next to bed.

21. Smell your clothes before bed, if you leave them out for the next day.

   a. Do you know what you're wearing tomorrow? Smell it.

   b. Notice if you clothes in the closet smell different than you expect.

   c. Notice if your favorite clothes smell different than you expect.

d. Notice if your clothes in the dryer smell different than you expect.

   e. Smell those same clothes in the morning.

      i. Do they smell the same?

      ii. If they smell differently, then you probably were abducted in those clothes.

22. Go to Bed.

23. Watch for signs. If you already know what these are, great. Try to remember as much as you can BEFORE the abduction.

   a. Are there shadows?

   b. Are there smoky things moving through your drapes?

   c. Do they come through windows or areas with windows?

   d. Can you describe the shape?

      i. Do you see them?

      ii. How do you know they are there?

      iii. Do you feel them?

      iv. Do you smell them?

      v. Is it Grays?

      vi. Mantis?

      vii. Others? Who? What?

   e. Cancel them!

   f. Write it down!

g. Lights? I found that a lot of lights were in my brain—programmed, if you will. To determine which is which, close your eyes.

   i. What do you see? Twinkling lights? Yep, me too. What this means, I have no idea. If you figure it out, let me know.

h. Do you see anything, feel anything? Remember these things for the next day.

i. If you feel a sting or whatever they use to knock you out, you know what to do:

   i. Cancellation tool!

   ii. Did you get the **Yes** or **No** signal?

   iii. If you get **No**, try again.

   iv. If you get a **Maybe**, add more qualifiers until you get a **Yes**.

   v. If you don't get a **Yes** write that down and go back to it later.

   vi. **Cancel** silently, in your mind. **Never cancel out loud**. They are listening. They want to know what you're thinking or what you know.

   vii. Information is power.

   viii. Information is currency.

24. If you see anything that you can draw, make a note to yourself to remember it, so that you can draw it in the morning.

25. If you feel fearful, or feel extreme negativity, try to remember, this is a fishing expedition for you to notice the signs of your abduction. You are watching them and you are taking notes and names for butt kicking later. I understand the fear. But to figure

this all out, you must treat them like an experiment. You are going to fall asleep eventually and we both know that.

   a. If you feel terrified, you can say **Yahweh**. **Yahweh** will clear a room quickly. Say it over and over, whisper it, sing it. You can do this out loud or in your head. It all works.

   b. **Ask your spirit guides for help.** I can feel the negativity of the room dissipate when I ask for help from my spirit guides.

   c. Say, "Spirit guides, please help! Please clear this room. Thank you. Thank you. Thank you."

26. When you wake up do you remember anything? For me, I see a black spot when I try to remember. This means a memory wipe. I came to this conclusion by remote viewing the black rectangle using *The Green Spiral Staircase* exercise in *The Hyperspace Helper* as an experiment and realized that all black rectangles for me, represents a memory wipe. It's a piece of my memory that is missing.

   a. What do you see?

      i. Remember it.

      ii. Write it down tomorrow.

27. Whenever you wake up from your abduction, immediately start up **LaHoChi**. When you start the healing positions, I hope you will fall asleep. I do. If you fall asleep **during** your **LaHoChi** session, this is ok. Your body may need this to happen so that you can heal.

28. In the morning,

   a. Grab your notebook

   b. Write down everything you remember. Even fragments.

   c. Smell your clothes.

d. Notice if you have extra hair on your face/under arms. Notice these things. You might have left for a week or longer! Because ETs bend time, no one notices you are gone but your body continues to age.*Note: bruises can take a while to show up on your body. When you notice them, document them in your notebook.

29. Let's get down to business:

    a. Get The Hyperspace Helper A User-Friendly Guide by Stewart A. Swerdlow and Janet D. Swerdlow

        i. Looking at your dreams or fragments, use the exercise called: *The Green Spiral Staircase* to **REMOTE VIEW** what is being kept from you.

        ii. Write it all down.

        iii. **Cancel** whatever is negative in it, which is all of it. Whatever you see.

        iv. If you have "dreams," they might be memories. They might be screen memories, given to you by the abductors. **Cancel** it all out! You have experience by now in what to do.

    b. Use each and EVERY exercise in the *Hyperspace Helper* book. You will need it. Follow the instructions for each exercise in this book.

    c. Get *Healing Archetypes & Symbols* by Stewart A. Swerdlow and Janet Diane Mourglia-Swerdlow and experiment with all of the other tools in this book. Some of them work better together. You will have to experiment on what works best for you. This book is very esoteric and was over my head when I first looked at it. But, you can figure it out.

30. Bruises on your body?

    a. ***Green Spiral Staircase***! Review what happened.

b. Cancel whomever and whatever did that to you.

31. It must be said that remote viewing is not an exact science. I use RV for clues and cancellation. Nothing more.

32. Take your notebook and pen with you on vacation. Write everything down that you do and what works and what doesn't work. Write down your dreams. Decipher the memories later. If epiphanies occur to you, write those down too. These things will help you get a picture of what is happening, why and who. I find it very important to figure this all out.

33. Do these same things each day. You will notice progress. It may take time. Don't give up. You will start to notice that you have fewer remote viewers or different ones or ….? In as little as two months I noticed a big difference. After a little while, patterns may emerge. You may know a little more of what's really going on. The truth.

34. If you are being abducted by people, use the same techniques. Reptilians? Same techniques. It is scary and dangerous, but I am SO angry that this is happening, that I do it anyway. Including this book.

    Note: They are watching us and they are adapting. You do that too. Also, there are more of them than us, so they can batter us with their numbers. Don't let that stop you. Be relentless, like they are. They can make our lives miserable, but they already are! So, what have we got to lose?

In Summary:

1. **Yahweh works for the first level of ETs.** I believe there are multiple layers: ETs, people and another layer I haven't quite figured out yet.

2. I put the **ultimate protection** on my calendar and renew it every two days. I add a **golden triangle** over it to make it stronger.

3. **Meditation and LaHoChi for healing**. Use meditation for comfort, healing, knowledge, relaxation. Being abducted and fearful is stressful. After every abduction, use **LaHoChi** on yourself. **This is very important**.

4. Use the **cancellation tool, with qualifiers.** For a typical day, if I feel pain, I cancel it, whether it's zaps to my toes, calf cramps, etc. I am **specific** in my cancellation.

    a. If I notice remote viewers, I cancel them, using the cancellation tool and qualifiers. **All remote viewers in all dimensions, all military personnel in all dimensions, according to the wishes of my oversoul and god-mind**. This can be exhausting because there are seemingly tons of remote viewers. But, don't give up. If you can keep at it, you should notice a difference in the types of abductions/abductors. When you see that, you are making progress toward ridding yourself of abductions.

5. **Dreams are real memories or screen memorie**s. Use cancellation. Screen memories are created by **us**. Our brains want to protect us from trauma and give us screen memories. They are not created by the abductor. *Communion,* by Whitley Strieber.

6. In these books you will find many helpful exercises. Use them all. Read the books.

7. When I use *The Hyperspace Helper*, I use every exercise in it, but not all at once. I use different exercises on different days. I don't want any cross contamination of thoughts. If I can remember what I saw in my last exercise, I try another.

8. Using these exercises in this book (any of them) will open you up to more info being revealed with meditation, "dreams," thoughts that pop into your heads, etc.

9. **Make up your own qualifiers**: new and old programming is a good one. Anything new or old because as soon as they change

something/your programming, it's new. Let your imagination run wild with the possibilities. Also, we are individuals and my qualifiers might not work for you and vice versa.

10. **Trust no one and no thing**. Check in with your oversoul and ask, "Is this entity good? Are they telling the truth?" If you do not get the positive signal—**CANCEL!**

Chapter 28
What I've Learned About Dreams

I have discovered that dreams can be in different forms. We have all heard that dreams have special meanings or everything in the dreams is you or everything in the dream is a symbol. For me, this has never been true. In the past, I knew that dreams felt like something, so when I had a "stress" dream, I was stressed. That's how I felt in the dream. After learning about screen memories, I have found that I am right. We all have had those dreams that we are in a class that we don't remember signing up for or dropping and today is the exam. Or, we lost our purse, wallet, our clothes and we are walking down the street naked. I now know to look at those dreams using the Green Spiral Staircase because when I have the "stress" dream, I know that I was being tortured or had a trauma that my mind is having a hard time dealing with. Look at your dreams. Do you have "stress" dreams, what are behind these dreams? Are some of them adventures? What were you really doing? This is important information. I've found that the type of dream you have will indicate the ET group you are with.

When you use the exercises like The Green Spiral Staircase, you open up your mind and the next night, information might pop in. Don't let the fear of being wrong about a theory stop you from investigating it. This is how you learn. This is how you put the puzzle pieces together.

Chapter 29
What I've Learned About Meditation

Someone said to me recently that they feel tingles in mediation and they thought this was "normal" and everyone feels tingles during meditation. You might think this too. Now, my question to you, is, "who, what, where, why, how?" If you feel tingles, who sent it to you? For what purpose? Where did it come from? Why did they send you tingles? How did they send you tingles? Is it normal to feel tingles during meditation? I don't think so. But, to be sure, use the cancellation tool. Because it may not be normal at all and it might not be to your benefit. Question everything you feel, see or hear.

Chapter 30
Abductors/ETs are Narcissists!

Narcissists are everywhere on Earth and have a very specific formulaic way of doing things. The ETs/abductors follow the narcissistic formula to a T.

My parents were both narcissists and I have a sister who is one as well. I had a horrible experience in 2016 with a malicious narcissistic neighbor who hacked my computer. My computer started acting strangely after I went out of town. I had a next-door neighbor's daughter checking on our cats and right after, my computer and my server—I am a former IT person—started having issues where items that I didn't open were left open on the server desktop as well as the computer desktop. I narrowed it down to that weekend and the neighbor and her daughter are computer illiterate, but my narcissistic neighbor worked for Booz Allen, the same agency where Edward Snowden worked and was a cloud expert, and knew a lot more about security than I did. Of course, I can't prove it was my narcissistic neighbor, but narcissists love to make your life miserable and make you wonder when the other shoe will drop. They also love to make sure you know they are much smarter than you are.

So, after having all sorts of problems with my computers, I discovered that I was hacked by a remote access Trojan, through Powershell, which is a native background program behind the graphical user interface where you can use command line tools to automate everything. This took me many months to figure out. What to do about it? I never figured that out because she is much more knowledgeable than I am—she turned my own computer against me using a native program. From what I could tell, she got an alert each time I logged into my computer on my home network. The only thing that stopped her, for a time, was to disconnect the server from the Ethernet. After rebuilding my desktop computer three times, I finally had to turn off my old server and rebuild my computer a fourth time. Now, I unplug my computer's Ethernet cable each and every time I use it. Yes, I had antivirus and antimalware, but how can those programs find a native to Windows program? They can't.

Being the person that I am, I read everything I could about people like my neighbor trying to identify her actions so that I could anticipate them and understand what happened. At first, I did not know what to call it—frenemy? Liar? I finally found a name for the way my neighbor was behaving: Narcissist. What was my neighbor doing to me? She was smearing me to my other neighbors. Telling them heinous stories that weren't true and since most of us give others the benefit of the doubt, they believed her without proof, without asking me. She was the victim. In truth, whatever she told them I did to her, she was doing to me.

During this investigation period I found and read multiple articles and books about narcissists, their disorder is called Narcissistic Personality Disorder (NPD). Normally NPD is a diagnosed mental health issue that people are treated for. But as with many mental health issues today, most narcissists are untreated, unchecked, undiagnosed and roam freely to destroy normal people's lives. In my case, most web articles were about romantic relationship narcissists, which is not what I was dealing with. It was hard to use the information I found for my situation. I wanted to understand my neighbor and know what I should do, shouldn't do, and what her next move would be.

Eventually, I found two exceptionally informative sites. One guy is on YouTube, and his channel is: BeGood4000. He does videos of the "demon narcissists." I learned so much from him and am SO thankful for his videos.

Another person who helped me, is a narcissist who goes by the pseudonym of HG Tudor. He is an author of multiple books about himself and other narcissists and he has a website: www.narcsite.com. He provides a service where anyone who is confused about narcissistic behavior can write to him, provide him with the situation, send him $40 via PayPal, and send him four questions. I did that. He wrote back and his analysis of the situation helped me understand what happened in my situation and why.

These experiences with narcissistic family members plus exceptional malicious narcissists were to prepare me for this book and making connections between what I'm seeing in my own family/experiences and the abductors.

Most articles on the web talk about a romantic relationship with a narcissistic man. Women are narcissists too, but they aren't talked about as much. However, I do see them in the news a lot more now.

Think about the narcissist in the news: A person who convinces another person to kill someone else based on the coercive and heinous stories the narcissist tells. The narcissist, self-absorbed and wanting money more than anything, wants some money from a life insurance policy and convinces someone else to kill their spouse because of the supposedly heinous activity. The narcissists are so convincing that people do not even QUESTION the veracity of their story. In normal instances, there is just shunning of the real victim of the narcissist. However, in extreme cases, if the narcissist gets their way, pressuring the individual and playing the victim to the max, the person in the way of their money gets killed.

Looking at the story with ETs you can see that a form of our government is working with ETs. The ETs need bodies for some reason. The government agrees to pretend not to know about the ETs and looks the other way. Anyone who gets in the way of the ETs or the government gets ruined. The abductees are isolated, abused, smeared if they talk, ETs convince the masses that anyone who is stating that they had negative experiences must be lying, because LOVE and ONENESS!

Now, look at a comparison of narcissists and ETs/abductors and see the similarities:

Human Narcissistic Behavior	ET/Abductor Behavior
Love Bombing – Making you believe you are special.	Love Bombing – They are learning from us. You are "chosen," you are "special." "You humans are so special that we need to learn from you continuously."
Mirroring – Drawing you in with similarities and fake stories (they may dress like you).	Mirroring—"You are helping us. We are helping each other. There's no one else like you who we can learn from. We are helping you know the oneness of the universe. LOVE!"
Smear Campaigns – Smear your character to everyone. Controlling the narrative about you to others.	Smear Campaigns – "If you go against us you are smeared. Your life is ruined. Negative stories about you abound. You can't make a living. You have to leave town. If we can't make you leave, we'll get your neighbors, your friends, your town to turn against you. We will turn everyone against you using heinous lies. We will besmirch your character. You are a liar."
Claiming they are the victim always.	Victimization – They claim they are doing their part to help us, but we aren't doing our part. This is victimization and projection. They can't help us until we show our willingness to help ourselves
If you fight back, the wrath of God is upon you.	ETs/Abductors punish you when they abduct you, that's why you have those bruises.
They isolate you as a way of control.	They control the narrative. You are afraid to talk to others because of fears of a ruined career, life, etc. This keeps you in line. You are fearful of talking about this with everyone. No one wants to be ridiculed by society by admitting this.
They physically abuse you and leave bruises as a way to control you.	You will find bruises, bumps, scars but have no way of knowing what happened.
Treat you anyway they want.	Your memory is erased so they can hide their dirty work.

Human Narcissistic Behavior	ET/Abductor Behavior
They are self-absorbed and image is everything.	Not taking responsibility: There is no such thing as a UFO. The government/military takes no responsibility. Who to complain to? Not me! That's someone else. Image is everything. This isn't BAD or negative. This is about LOVE and ONENESS. Those talking about us in a negative way are liars.
Gaslighting. They have you questioning your sanity about events that happened.	Make sure you have no idea what is true and what isn't. Make sure everything has a GRAIN of truth. It's true in a way. You could "say" it's TRUE. This never happened. You dreamt it. Dreams have special meanings and everything in a dream is you. Or, everything in a dream has a definition and it means something else. Conflicting information.
Using proxies/flying monkeys to do their dirty work. So, even if they have left the scene, someone else has taken up the cause, relentlessly. Flying monkeys by definition are people who act on behalf of a narcissist to a third party, usually for an abusive purpose.	Proxies/Flying Monkeys. Military, other abductors play the game, relentlessly for the ETs.
The Discard. If they discard you, the smear campaign starts. If you discard them, all hell breaks loose. Narcissistic rage.	This book is about discarding the ET. Like a narcissist, they will fight, they will discredit. They will do dirty tricks. They will up the ante and do anything they can to get you back in their clutches. While I was writing this book, The ETs made changes to my document, some were small, some changes were giant deletions. They will get you back for daring to walk away from them.
Fuel – the lifeblood of the narcissist. Fuel is any emotional response to something they have said, done or caused. A narcissist enjoys hurting us and creating chaos in our lives. This is their agenda, and fuel is their purpose for living and hurting us.	Fuel. The ET agenda is to hurt us so that they can have fuel from our pain. They torture us over and over with painful procedures and experiments so that they can feel good. This is their agenda. They take us not for altruism, but instead for fuel.

This is not an exhaustive list of narcissistic tendencies, but I wanted you to see the similarities in their behaviors, so that you look at them and can anticipate what they will do next.

Narcissists discard, and if you discard them they have narcissistic rage. The ET's get furious when you try to leave their grasp. They punish you and you will get stress dreams—this is the punishment for trying to leave them. It is my belief that we go through horrific trauma and with their technology, they put us back together, so they can do it again the next night. They get off on hurting us.

Looking back on my situation with my narcissistic neighbor, I can see how she hooked me. She told me no one liked her in the neighborhood. I felt sorry for her and tried to put myself in her shoes. It didn't set off any alarm bells, as it should have. She was being a victim, to hook me. Later, she plied me with wine and probed me for information about myself and the neighborhood in the vein of "getting to know me." She also told me how similar we were, because we worked in similar jobs, and were career women. Immediately, within a month of meeting me, she started courting others for friendship, and maligning me to others, to set the stage for the smear campaign.

Once the smear campaign starts, there is nothing you, as the smeared, can do. Narcissists are jealous of everything. You might have a nicer car, the smear happens, you might have more money, then the smear. But the point is that they control the narrative—that is the point. The ETs/military control the narrative of abductions, like the narcissist who controls the narrative of the smear on you. Because the narcissist is an effective and cunning liar, they have gained the trust and sympathy of everyone around you. They are projecting their own actions onto you. You're doing it to them. What does this do? Fear. Everyone is afraid to be on the narcissist's bad side. She is controlling everyone around you, against you. She also makes sure she has others working for her—a smear campaign requires flying monkeys or proxies who are people that the narcissist trusts to keep control of her narrative.

I put this personal information about narcissists and myself in this book so that you would know I studied how narcissism works and you would be able to spot the human narcissists and make the correlation between narcissistic ET or military abductors.

Hopefully this information will help you connect the dots when you cross paths with a narcissist—human, ET, or military—in your own life, like my crazy neighbor.

The abductions are all about control. Control is key.

The ETs control the narrative. They claim that they are really helping us. But, they still ERASE our MEMORIES! If they have nothing to hide, and are doing good things, why erase our memories?

What are they really doing? They are taking away our choices. They are **choosing** the narrative for us and not allowing us to come to our own conclusions.

What is their true agenda?

Chapter 31
Deceptions of the ETs/Military

Cloaking: Cloaking is a vibration as well as an invisibility device that they use against us. It is something done deliberately. When the abductors cloak, they might change their vibration so that it seems friendly, warm, neutral. Be aware of this. Cloaking is an intentional act. It can be vibrational misinformation. If you are ever fooled by anyone or anything that's why. It might be that they are vibrationally different and you simply can't see them. Regardless if it is intentional, or even programmed, we can't see them, and they know it. Remember, the problem is not us, we have done nothing wrong; it is something they're doing to us so we can't see them.

Reincarnation is a SCAM. The Earth is an illusion of safety. Our "free will" comes at a cost.

We are told (1) we chose this life before we were born, (2) we are here to learn lessons, (3) we choose to go to the light and (4) we have free will. That's the beauty of it all.

Being narcissistic in their ways, the ETs are giving us a grain of truth. The ETs control the human body. They own it. When we die—the propaganda tells us to "go to the light." Movies tell us this, books, etc. Did you know that the US government has a liaison of movie approval? This department deals with approving military movies. Is it such a stretch that this department could also approve other movies that shape our perceptions?

As they say, "going to the LIGHT" is our CHOICE. It is my belief that the TRUTH is that choosing the LIGHT puts us back onto the Earth, into SLAVERY. Think about it. If everyone dies and gets recycled continuously, we can be told, we CHOSE and they have a ready supply of victims to experiment on, etc. They claim we have FREE WILL. They don't tell us there is another choice.

It turns out the OTHER CHOICE when the LIGHT turns on is to say: **"I want to go home."**

We can fix this, **choose to go home**. The LIGHT is a trick to reincarnation, so we can come back here to do this all over again. This is how we CHOOSE our contracts of slavery with the ETs. Does that sound like a CHOICE to you? It's a trick. It's fake. It's propaganda.

This makes so much sense to me now that I look back on my remote view of a Reptilian saying to me **"I own you, you don't own you. I'm in charge, you're not in charge."** Slavery.

I'm a slave and so are you. Everyone on Earth is a slave. Our SOULS are stuck in our bodies and are slaves. Our souls are not from Earth only our bodies are from Earth. This is the TRUTH.

When loved ones die, tell them to ask to go home. If they go to the light they are reincarnated. Being here is slavery.

My father passed in April of this year. Before his soul left, I told him to say, "I want to go home," and not go to the light. After he passed and a few days later, I had a dream that I was carrying him and he was wearing just a shirt. I carried him to a cave and cut off his clothes. The shirt was sewn onto him, meaning he could not take it off. I was told this was slavery—the slaves could not remove their clothes. That's how you could distinguish slaves from non-slaves. I helped release him by giving him the information to say, "I want to go home."

Love and Oneness. A lot of ETs show their abductees the wonderment of being abducted. They manipulate their emotions. They "show" them how it's all connected. It's wonderful! This is **propaganda**. They tell other abductees "you are special." You are "chosen." This is part of the illusion that these other people are in a special project. This is about the ETs "learning" about us. It's altruistic. We were chosen. It makes us feel special. It's all slavery. They want your buy in. They want the masses to buy in and to stay on the Earth.

I'm not saying LOVE and ONENESS is not a truth. I'm saying that the ETs are using it against us to keep us from figuring out what they are really doing. It's a cover for the truth. They are manipulating us by using LOVE and LIGHT as a manipulation tool. They are using our belief system against us. What are they hiding? We should all be asking ourselves this question.

This is a war for the souls. This is not a game. I have been told multiple times by different people that our time on Earth is a "game." It's a war. Our souls are fighting for freedom from the ET AGENDA, which is SLAVERY. I'm not saying that's the only agenda, but it is one of them. We are at WAR. Our souls are fighting to remember and leave this planet.

Don't go to the light, because if you do, you will be reincarnated and sent back to Earth to have another life and continue to be enslaved by ETs. Tell all of your loved ones.

In meditation, you are communicating with your SOUL. When you receive messages from your soul, the abductors cannot stop this. They can't know what you know and what you've been told by your soul unless YOU tell them. If you share what your soul communicates to another person, ETs will hear it. I believe that meditation gets around programming.

The ETs/military people control our bodies. Have you ever had a zap on your toe or a pain that suddenly occurs? I have and I started **cancelling** it out each time it happens. And it disappears. Try it. Since I am older now, I've started getting zaps on my feet at night. Common knowledge would tell you that this is diabetes and it is the start of peripheral neuropathy. One night when it was happening to me, a zap on the ball of my foot, I thought—what if this is a programming situation—i.e., the abductors are causing this zap. Could I stop it? The answer is **Yes!** I cancelled out this zap. I said to myself, in my head, "I now 'brown x' out all unnecessary negativity in my life. I now 'brown x' out all that is zapping my left foot right now." That zapping/electricity feeling stopped. After that, I wrote down and tried out my newfound knowledge by "brown xing" out everything that I felt was possibly negative. Now, recognize that I don't know if it's me [my body] or someone else [hurting me], and I don't have to. Stewart Swerdlow's book taught me that the oversoul will tell me if this "experience" is necessary or unnecessary for me. I have to wonder what else is unnecessary negativity? Think about yourself—do you have any aches and pains that you could try to "brown x" out and see if you can stop them? If so, what could this mean? Do you have to suffer these aches and pains? If your oversoul says yes, when you "brown x" out something, then the obstacle is removed from your journey. If your oversoul says no, then, it must remain. Think about the possibilities.

Chapter 32
My Experiences
2017

Disclaimer: remote viewing is not 100% accurate. I use these dreams and remote views as tools/clues.

These experiences are notes from my journal/notebooks that I write on each day after my experiences overnight. All of you should be doing this too. It helps to reflect, and you can write down everything you figure out. I wrote down everything that could possibly be data. So, I did write down times when I woke up. This was just me trying to figure out what was important and what was not and I had no idea if time of night was important.

Note: in 2017 I was working with a medium, trying out different "groups" who could help me with my "abduction contracts." Some of them were "Ashtar Space Command, Arturians, Pleiadians." At this time, I had no idea if it would work, so I tried everything.

I was also told by my medium to ask three times "Are you from the light? Are you from love? Are you from God?" to determine if someone was "good" or "from the light." If they passed the "test," then they were good and I should "feel" their goodness. I never did.

Other times when I say I was told, it means that my spirit guides gave me the information.

1/30/17 Message from spirit guides. We are preparing you not just for mediumship but to be a warrior.

2/1/17 – 7/8/17 Working on becoming a medium.

7/8/17 Dream. Had a dream about a dark being with long pointy fingernails that cut my heel and cut out a piece of skin. **This was real**. There was a round piece of skin missing from my heel.

7/19/17 Medium sent me an ET intervention. Practicing saying: "I am the sun, divine light, sovereign being."

8/5/17 Dream. Dream about a small pinecone removed from my ear.

8/5/17 Acupuncturist visit. Went to the acupuncturist and he said I do remote viewing and it hasn't been turned off and that's why my 10-year-old self had the same daydream every day for a week and then it came true. This was remote viewing. He thinks remote viewing is the tip of the iceberg.

8/6/17 Before sleep. Heard a low-flying plane, a helicopter and the pulsing of a ship of some type. I then heard footsteps on the roof and then a sound like someone coming through the windows. I didn't see anything but I did see shadows—several beings congregated up on the ceiling. I tried to get rid of them and asked my angels and support teams to get rid of them. They couldn't do it.- I asked the shadows why they were all here and they said, "You fascinate us." I hear the low-flying plane and the helicopter regularly each time I get taken. This time was different. This time I saw a shadow of a Praying Mantis near my bed around six to seven feet tall. As I was lying there, I felt a sting on my right thigh and then a smack to my lady parts as if it was hit by a spoon or a tuning fork. It hurt. Then I saw the Mantis point at me and I felt an overwhelming desire to sleep. I fought it but eventually did sleep. I woke up at 2:25 AM.

8/13/17 After sleep. Couldn't sleep right away, but fell asleep around 4 AM. Had two nightmares about spiders. One dream was about two spiders fighting and another was about a small spider with long legs. Later, I had a sensation of having wet sinuses and ears. Like I was underwater. I had the distinct impression of drying out, like sand. When my sinuses were wet it felt uncomfortable like the feeling of having water up your nose.

8/15/17 Before sleep. Went to bed around 1 AM. After healing, felt negativity. So, I respectfully demanded my support team

(Archangel Michael, Violet Flame, Arturian Council of Light and Pleiadian Council of Light) to intervene and get rid of them NOW. They did. The bedroom cleared out. Koreg then mentioned that just because the other entities' were "neutral" didn't mean they could stay. I agreed and asked the support team to get rid of the neutral entities and that only those of love and light could stay. I felt better.

8/18/17 Saw my medium. I'm supposed to switch over from being experimented on to working with Commander Ashtar. I am not an ambassador, but a gatekeeper keeping a portal open for other people like me, to get through.

8/17/17 Before sleep. I felt a spider arm touching my head last night and I freaked out a bit, calling my support team and asking them to make whatever was touching me, leave. They couldn't because it was a praying mantis of love and light, named MOMA. I told Ashtar Command that I was ready to switch from being experimented on to whatever I was supposed to do. Apparently, MOMA was here to say goodbye and I didn't understand her actions and she was taken aback with my reactions. I had to ask her if she was from LOVE, LIGHT and GOD three times. She passed the test.

8/20/17 Before sleep. Felt the terrible anguish. Koreg said it was MOMA.

8/21/17 Before sleep. Told MOMA I was so sorry for hurting her feelings with my ignorance and said that she could visit me anytime she wanted and the other Mantises as well who were always on my ceiling and that I didn't know and I would work on our relationship. That feeling of anguish went away.

8/23/17 Before sleep. I felt something touch my right leg. It had been hurting, throbbing. I had a run in with a recycle bin. It was MOMA. She said she could work on my leg but would have to take me to her ship. I felt wary of being taken on a ship and said so. MOMA is from the light but I was still scared. She asked, "What if the bad guys take you—can I take you from them to my ship and heal your leg? Is that alright?" I said yes. I told her I was sorry and this relationship was new but I know we can build trust. I woke up this morning and my right leg feels much better! When I met MOMA, I felt like she was a motherly figure. Maybe assigned to me when I was a child and has cared for me all this time. The anguish I felt was strong and agonizing. I felt so bad.

8/24/17 Awake. Three weird things happened last night. (1) After MOMA was in my room last night and I felt she was a motherly presence, BUT she wanted me to agree to let her take me to her ship. I said I had doubts so that meant NO for now. Uncertainty for me = do nothing. She left. I also said to her, "I can't remember anything, so it is hard to trust." (2) I woke up to a really loud tone in my right ear, then I heard a color. A large glowing white stripe appeared close to my right ear. It got bigger, brighter and louder. I started saying/screaming "OH NO, OH NO." (3) Heard a large vehicle leaving at 5 AM. Felt like I was back in my own bed. After going to the acupuncturist, I think my throbbing leg was signaling MOMA to come and see me. The acupuncturist said that any "convincing" was against free will and is probably a trick! Yikes! Glad I didn't fall for it.

8/26/17 Thoughts. After some thinking on it, I think the whole MOMA thing was a manipulation. The name MOMA could have been a MOM/MAMA combo to make me think of a motherly figure. They could manipulate my feelings of anguish like I hurt her feelings as well as a motherly feeling, but they could not manipulate my free will and that's why it felt NEUTRAL and I would have to give them permission. Why they are so desperate to get me on their ship is beyond me right now. Hopefully, I will figure that out soon. I also wonder if there are multiple implants in my body each representing a different group. I don't know why or how the one in my leg turned on. I'm glad it's turned off.

8/28/17 Thoughts. Woke up in the middle of the night completely soaked and stuck to the bed. Sheets were all wet, the pillow was wet. Had to put the sheet on top and go back to sleep. Had multiple dreams but one dream was badly stitched together like I was stitched into it and the seam was showing. One thing that was strange was that Bob woke up with my lipstick on the top of his cuticle on his index finger. Did he do that to trigger a memory of being taken? Did I do that to trigger both of us?

8/30/17 After sleep. Woke up with long scratch on my right forearm. It's about 1.5 inches. This morning and yesterday morning I felt there was a problem underneath the dreams that I was trying to solve. This has happened before. Today's was a problem I was trying to solve. The other has been something about how I can't turn on the lights or something about lights being bad or lights will alert them. I don't know what that means. This is always running in the background of my dreams like the dreams are overlaid over the problem I'm trying to solve in order to obscure it.

8/30/17 Awake. Today at 4 PM. I heard a male voice in my head, telling me this was the US government. They said I have a gift and I gave them permission to be in my head. I didn't believe them so I told him to call me on my phone(s) since they have my numbers. No one called. They told me that they've known about my gift since I was a little girl and said they could have pulled that out of my memory banks. That's when I had the idea for them to call my phone. It's weird and obviously has to do with remote viewing since I'm reading about a guy who does that right now. I also told them to get the hell out of my head! Who do they think they are?? I have found my power.

8/31/17 Dream. Had a dream about my mother. We were in the dining room of her house. Mom was wearing navy blue and she looked like her normal self. She said she was worried about Sarah (my sister). Worried about Sarah's health.

8/31/17 I texted Sarah about her health. I texted Sarah and said, "I had a dream. Mom was in it. She is worried about your health—what's going on with your health?" Sarah said, "Mom is a tattletale!" Sarah was having trouble with her blood pressure spiking.

10/2/17 Awake. The light in my eye turned on and I closed my eye. I don't trust it anymore. I also saw a white pointed patch of light that appeared from a window blind. Koreg said I am awakening.

I had no idea this is what was meant by "awakening."

10/2/17 Before sleep. I saw geometric shapes overlapping in red, brown, and black in my room.

10/6 – 10/7/17 Went to bed late at 1 AM. Heard a low-flying plane and I knew they were already here. My eyeball went off, brightly circling my eye. I heard noises in the bedroom. I stated, "I consciously, unconsciously, subconsciously say NO!" I also respectfully demanded from the Pleiadian Council of Light to get them out of my room. I felt negativity and saw a lot of beings on the ceiling. After stating NO and asking everyone to leave, I felt better—no negativity. Then, I tried to stay awake as long as I could. Fell asleep around 2:15 AM.

10/7/17 Started reading *Healing Archetypes & Symbols* by Stewart A. Swerdlow and Janet Diane Mourglia-Swerdlow, and *The Hyperspace Helper A User Friendly Guide* also by Stewart A. Swerdlow and Janet D. Swerdlow.

10/14/17 Before sleep. Felt one needle sting on my left thigh.

10/15/17 After abduction. Woke up with square needle marks on right upper arm. I took pictures. **I now know these are stun gun marks.**

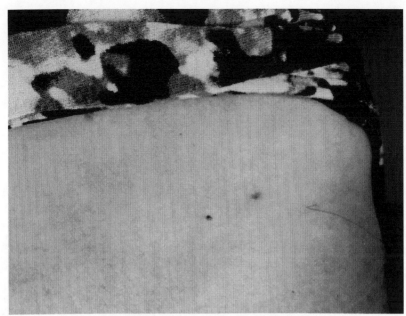
Upper right arm stun gun marks.

10/17/17 After abduction. Woke up at 1:40 AM. Felt like I was disoriented and looking around a room—a huge black cave with fires around the ceiling or lights. It was a huge hollow room. I've been there before. My right eye was burning and cold like it had been open for a while. At 3:59 AM I woke up to my cat meowing. I left my bed and this seemed to satisfy her. I heard movement and rushing around from the bedroom. 12:34 AM is the last time I remember looking at the clock, but "they" were already in the room since 11:43 PM waiting for me to fall asleep. I also found a bump with the skin scrapped off and a very thin line moving away from it. It looks like an incision or scar that is hard to see and you can just barely feel it. Very weird. To feel the line on my stomach, you must rub your finger horizontally, away from the bump.

10/18/17 Dream. Dreamt that I was taking a packet of powder and in not enough water. It didn't taste good.

10/18/17 Before sleep. With five low-flying planes, I could hear them in my room by 11:43 PM. I was awake until 12:15 AM. I saw the gaggle of Praying Mantises on the ceiling, watching. I then asked Archangel Michael, Pleiadian Council of Light, and Spirit Guide Council to remove all negative entities RIGHT NOW! Decided to try using **cancellation** as long as the oversoul and God-mind agreed (per the Swerdlows' *Healing Archetype & Symbols* book).

10/19/17 Before sleep. Before sleeping last night, I saw a grid. It was clear like I was looking through glass—like a ladder with different colors on the grid showing some symbols. The background was slate blue and POOF! It disappeared in white smoke. The ladder was an "H" on its side, an "N" on its side and an "I." The "H" was red and the "I" was orange. I drew this, but it's hard to explain.

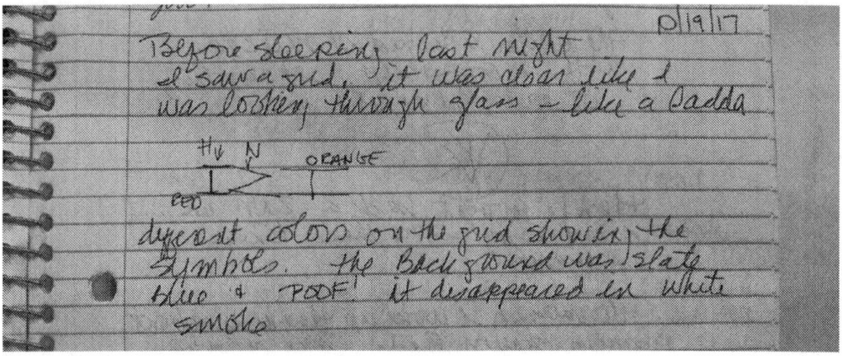

[Handwritten journal excerpt dated 10/19/17 reproducing the above text with a sketch of the H, N, and I symbols labeled with colors.]

10/20/17 Before sleep. Heard one low-flying plane at 11:45 PM. Thought they were in the room because I heard the noises that precede them.

10/21/17 Dream. Cloudy skies and several pairs of flying vehicles in the sky. They looked like a cannon flying around in formation in pairs. People were scared. One little ship flew into a window and asked me my name. I said "Lisa O'Hara" and it told me that I was not in service just yet. This vehicle asked the guy next to me and he wouldn't tell them his real name. First he gave initials like "CG" and then "Fly fly." It kept asking. He seemed afraid.

> Had 2 Dreams.
> (1) Cloudy skies + Multiple z's flying vehicles in the sky.
> [box] + [shape] + OTHERS I can't remember. They were flying around + people were scared. One little fly flew into a window + asked me my name. I said "Elizabeth O'Hara" + it told me I was not in service just yet. This fly asked a guy next to me + he wouldn't tell them his real name - just he gave initials - like "YG", then "fly fly". It kept asking. He seemed afraid.

10/22/17 Dream. Woke up at 6 AM dreaming about standing in a line and seeing the name KOOZLE. **Is this a code word for a mission?**

10/24/17 Woke up three times at 12:30 AM. This is a time slip.

10/25/17 Dream. I was in a hotel room and had long black hair with ½ of a pink tiara. In this dream, I heard a tone in my ear and screamed because they were coming.

10/29/17 Awake. Heard infernal beeping/Morse code while a refrigerator was running. Decided to record it. Recorder on phone would not start and beeping stopped. AHA!

10/31/17 Awake. Hear this beeping in the vent of our master bathroom and I think they conceal it in various normal appliance noises.

11/6/17 Before sleep. Heard two low-flying planes. Woke up at 3 AM to a cat sound, a scratchy meow. It didn't sound like either cats. Heard someone say, "Things are moving, you just don't know it," twice.

11/8/17 Before sleep. Heard three low-flying planes plus helicopters. Woke up at 3 AM, 4 AM and 6:30 AM. I felt hot each time.

11/9/17 Before sleep. Had a hard time sleeping. Heard low-flying planes plus helicopters. The low-flying planes were at 11:40 PM, 12:23 AM and 12:31 AM. At 2 AM I saw some big red billowing smoke coming in through the middle of the curtains that spread across the entire south side of the room. A battle occurred. Apparently, it was some beings and Koreg, my guide, was protecting me against whoever else wanted me.

11/10/17 After sleep. I heard that fake bird again and then thought about Blue Avians. Koreg then told me that the bird sounds were him and other Blue Avians and they were there whenever I needed protection. Since I heard the fake bird noises at 4 PM one time, he told me they wanted me to make the connection between Blue Avians and birds at a time where I was completely awake. So, whenever I hear them, they are protecting me. They told me to worry about my mission and they will worry about protecting me.

11/11/17 Dream. Had a dream about going shopping and the store was 100 elevator stops underground but they had the best cake ever. So, we went. There were some strange people. One had no clothes on and no butt cheeks—just a hole in the back.

11/12/17 Dream. I had a dream about looking at a map. The map was a squiggled line with a circle on parts of the squiggle. Each time I heard low-flying plane, the dream would reset and I would be back looking at a map. It reset about five times.

11/17/17 Before sleep. Two low-flying planes. One at 11 PM, one at 1:30 AM. Fell asleep around 3:30 AM. I am being physically taken or leaving my bed. When I get back I have physical bruises and I get really hot each time I return. I woke up at 6:30 AM and felt dread at knowing what really happened—that I can't remember.

11/17/17 After sleep. My gums on the front teeth at the top has a huge blister. It wasn't there before I went to bed. It hurts on the very top of my gums, near my nose. The bruises on the inside of my forearms are distinct and 2 inches to 2.5 inches apart, vertical to my forearm, towards my hand.

11/18/17 – 11/19/17 Before sleep. Heard ship land on house around 2 AM. Tried to stay awake. Made it until 4:30 AM. I was taken. Had bruises.

11/20/19 Dream. Had a dream about working at a job. My nameplate said LISA WILL. It was new and just made in block lettering.

11/21/17 Dream. Had a dream about Bob. He was wearing all black and we both were working at a company called NASIENT. We lived in an apartment complex and there was a storm and all of the cars were floating in the water except ours because we had it parked on higher ground close to the building. Bob had been there a week already and everyone knew everything about me.

11/24/17 Before sleep. Low-flying plane 10:30 PM.

11/28/17 Dream. Woke up suddenly at 12:20 AM. Didn't know where I was. Didn't know if Bob was in bed with me. Checked—he wasn't there. No sounds. Very dark. There were zig zags on the ceiling above me. Finally realized Bob was there.

11/29/17 Dream. Had a horrifying dream. I was a pregnant woman. I was in a facility but it was dark, and it was hard to see faces. I felt like I knew the people down the hall from my large room. There was another room with men I recognized as colleagues. I was in bed and falling out of bed as a person/entity felt up my back, looking for a hole, up my spine, all the way up to my head. When the person could not find the hole, they put their hand in my mouth and twirled it around in my throat telling me I had no tonsils (this is true). I woke up suddenly with a dry throat.

12/2/17 Before sleep. Someone named Lieutenant Granger told me I needed to go to bed because I had work to do. He was from the light but Granger was not his real name. He told me I didn't want to know and it was better that way.

12/3/17 Before sleep. Two low-flying planes. One at 11:15 PM. And another at 11:25 PM.

12/4/17 Before sleep. Helicopter at 12:25 AM.

12/4/17 Slept fitfully. Kept waking up screaming or screaming in my dream. At one point there was a BIG WHITE LIGHT over my bed and I thought "SOURCE" and then I vibrated all over for a while. I was unsure of time. I woke up every few minutes—1:56 AM, 2:06 AM, 2:15 AM, 3:33 AM, 5:06 AM, and then 8 AM and I knew I was safe because it was light. Between 8 – 9:15 AM I had a dream about getting a flat tire and having some people, including Bob, help me with it. Koreg told me that the white light was a source attunement.

12/5/17 Before sleep. Heard three low-flying planes, 1:19 AM, 2:31 AM and 3:06 AM Heard the room making weird noises and I couldn't sleep. Felt a presence near my bed, watching me. It made me uneasy but not scared.

12/6/17 Before sleep. One low-flying plane at 10:30 PM low-flying plane at 11:50 PM.

12/21/17 Before sleep. 12:21 AM low-flying plane.

12/22/17 Before sleep. Heard one low-flying plane at 12:21 AM and woke up suddenly at 1:15 AM and felt electricity all around or on me. Woke up at 2:15 AM and felt it again.

12/29/17 Before sleep. My spirit guide Koreg told me some of the marks on my body (bruises) were made by tools for inoculation and some by torture devices. He couldn't tell me more but said that disclosure was going to happen soon in each timeline and had in fact, already started with cigar-shaped ship and emergency "satellites" put in space by US and different countries. He said I would have enough time to learn remote viewing if I applied myself.

12/31/17 Before sleep. One low-flying plane at 12 midnight.

Chapter 31
My Experiences
2018

I use LaHoChi each and every time I wake up. Even if I didn't put it in my journal, I use it. So, as you read my journal, it goes without saying that I used LaHoChi.

1/2/18 After sleep. I woke up at 1:38 AM with a start and saw lights of green/yellow, and 1:38 AM in digital numbers everywhere around the room. I woke up at 6:02 AM to go to the bathroom. Usually, I wake up at 6:48 AM.

1/3/18 Before sleep. I could hear a ship waiting for me to sleep. As I was falling asleep, I became afraid. There was no fear until the end of awakeness. Not sure if it was fear of the unknown, fear of the known, or excitement. Woke up at 5:09 AM.

1/3/18 Dream Multiple dreams about being a nurse, instead of RN, the initials were LMK. I wore a badge around my neck and was helping out with two surgeries in a big room with plastic surrounding it. Two people walked in and I told them to wait outside. I was needed in two surgeries at the same time. I had a walkie talkie to talk to the surgeons and to run back and forth. I also spent some time at the beach. At one point during the surgery I had to go back to the desk and my credentials were questioned. I showed them my badge LMK which meant I was an RN.

1/7/18 Before sleep. One helicopter at 1:30 AM one low-flying plane at 1:50 AM.

1/11/18 Before sleep. One low-flying plane 11:55 PM.

1/14/18 After sleep. Koreg said the beings watch us like a show. Like we are in a zoo. He also said that the chem trails block the energy coming from the sun and other beings to awaken us all. I was given a suggestion to purchase an air purifier and I did it. He said that I am affecting everyone like a drop of water in a pond and I am a beacon of light, drawing the beings to me. It is not a coincidence that the planes go over my house trying to block the energy I put out.

1/16/18 Before sleep. Was told that injuries from human/Reptilian = pain. Injuries from ET = no pain. 11:51 PM one low-flying plane, 11:56 PM one low-flying plane.

1/17/18 Before sleep. 12:12 AM one low-flying plane, 12:20 AM one low-flying plane.

1/19/18 Before sleep. 11:45 PM one low-flying plane, 11:52 PM one low-flying plane.

1/23/18 Before sleep. One low-flying plane 1:09 AM.

1/25/18 Before sleep. 12:45 AM one low-flying plane. Woke up with bruise on inner right thigh.

1/2/18 Before sleep. One low-flying plane 12:52 AM.

1/27/18 Dream Had a dream about repeating five minutes of time. I was on a task and it was my job to go back in time and repeat those five minutes. It seems like I did repeat the same five minutes multiple times.

2/6/18 Before sleep. Was told remote viewing and the unconscious mind is the key by my guides.

2/11/18 Before sleep. At 3:30 AM felt my room get tense. I then saw a movement of black near the door. Then the room felt menacing. I heard a lot of sounds of beings in my room. I respectfully demanded Archangel Michael make them leave. They didn't go. Then Koreg gave me the idea of sage spray and I sprayed the room but felt them still in the bathroom. I was too tired to sage bathroom. Fell asleep.

2/12/18 Before sleep. Koreg said I did all the right things and the "shadow people" did not expect me to notice their presence and that's why it went from tense to menacing. And they helped Koreg and the spirit guides out with something but they can't tell me what it is.

2/15/18 12:04 AM low-flying plane. Woke up at 1:45 AM saying to myself: **"Camp 142."**

2/17/18 Dream. Had a dream about working in a computer data center with one other guy. He was telling people that they were not getting paid. There was a big tall bank of computers (black) with green and yellow digital numbers. I was getting paid because I worked many days straight.

2/21/18 Before sleep. 10:56 PM one low-flying plane, 10:58 PM one low-flying plane, 11:14 PM one helicopter. Woke up at 2:14 AM, woke up at 5 AM and 6:30 AM. Had a dream about a guy who had his own language but it sounded like English but with growling in it. I could understand it. The guy had an odd shaped head with big hair. He was orange.

2/23/18 Dream. I was driving our car around a town. I needed to turn around and I made a maneuver that I would never make in real life. I turned into a small street and turned and then I was out of the car and walking/climbing on a rocky area. I knew I was dreaming so I said, "I want to see my car down the street so I can drive, not climb." **But, my car did not appear, indicating to me that this was REAL, not a dream.** However, on the rocky cliff, two wolves appeared. They weren't scary and got close to me. The wolves took me to a house. It was very small inside and narrow with a low ceiling. A person met us at the door, he had no hair and had two orange faces, one in front and one on the back of his head. His faces were smooth. He was taking me to someone. Everyone in that house had completely smooth and kind of wet and shiny faces. Multiple people were walking me around the house to a room where someone was waiting for me. The house had low ceilings and very narrow walls and it looked like a maze and was claustrophobic in there. I think this house was underground.

2/26/18 Before sleep. 11:37 PM one low-flying plane and at 11:40 PM one low-flying plane.

2/27/18 Before sleep. 12:45 AM, one low-flying plane, 4:11 AM one low-flying plane.

2/28/18 After sleep. Woke up at 6:30 AM with a film over my eyes like tic tac toe with 000 00. It was a specific design.

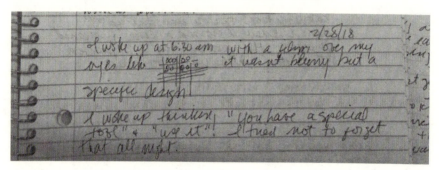

3/2/18 Dream. I had applied at the FBI. The background check would cost $5,000. It was a lot and several people and I discussed it. I was on the phone talking to a woman. **(this is monumental—I can never hear anything on a phone in a dream—I always wake up knowing it's a dream because no one ever answers—was this a dream or real?)** I could hear her talking to others and some static saying I'd passed some tests. Then she said I had to go to 455 Battery Street in San Francisco and do an "intercept" with an alien being. I would know/realize/recognize this being when I saw it. I was wondering why I had applied since I am 56 years old and thought in 20 years I'd be 76, having put in my 20 years. I was wondering if I'd made a mistake when she asked me, "How many times have you killed yourself?" I replied, "More that I know of." The woman's voice was very clear. I had applied with another guy and we discussed the cost of the background checks of $5000 being high. I woke up with the song "Hold Me" in my head by Fleetwood Mac.

3/5/18 Found a red mark on my butt on the right side near my thigh. It hurts. I also found that my gel nail polish was disturbed on the right side of my left index finger. It's like someone tried to take the polish off. I went back to gel after taking a six-month hiatus. My spirit guides told me to stop putting it on so I did. After a while, six months, I really missed it and put it back on and now I'm getting the feeling that I need to stop again. I need a REASON! So, I hope someone is listening.

3/6/18 Before sleep. There was an entity in my room. I heard it before I saw it. It didn't feel menacing. It made clicking noises sometimes but mostly quiet. I asked to see it and I saw a big cloud of green fog. 11:24 PM, one helicopter and one plane or ship that landed on roof.

3/14/18 After sleep. Woke up at 2:44 AM to lights near the curtains on my side of the bed that looked like several vertical cursive capital letter "L." Next time I will get up and investigate.

3/18/18 After sleep. Went to bed at 1:22 AM, I woke up around 2:30 AM. I woke myself up trying to scream but being unable to and there was negativity—a lot of it. Damn aliens! After I went to the bathroom, I came back and tried to sleep and the negativity was back so I said in my head "I AM THE SUN!" Multiple times until the negative aliens went away. I hope I FRIED their instruments of terror and them! Bastards!

3/21/18 9:30 PM one low-flying helicopter, 12:31 AM one low-flying plane. Had a dream about talking to a neighbor on the phone. I could hear her!! **This is the second time I've been able to hear someone on the phone. Usually I realize it's a dream because there is no one on the line that I can hear.** Progress.

3/28/18 While transcribing my medium's session for 3/23/18, I saw to the right of my computer a face on the wall. It was clear with outlines. I just saw it quickly out of the corner of my eye and then it popped and was gone!

3/30/18 Dream. I saw a screen that was black, like a DOS screen and someone was reprogramming me. The typing was very small and I saw the screen moving away from me and getting smaller and smaller. I couldn't see what was being done. The area around the screen was blue.

3/31/18 Woke up with a big scratch on the inside of my left arm, near the elbow and near a vein. It looks like a scratch from a cat but it doesn't hurt or sting even when I put water on it.

4/1/18 Saw four Praying Mantises with brown robes on in the den. It was a flash. A second of the image.

4/2/18 Discovered that my server, a Windows2008R2 server, has been compromised with a remote access Trojan. I discovered this because I started noticing that my Windows 7 computer was acting strangely and dialog boxes were open that I didn't open. My computer does strange things. It's been going on for a while. I was trying to figure out what was going on. How did someone remotely access my server? I disconnected it from the network a few times to try to troubleshoot which computer was the culprit. It was my server. When my server was unplugged from the network, everything seemed fine. No weird issues with my computer. This is either a remote access Trojan or a PowerShell hack. PowerShell is a Windows programming tool behind the graphical user interface. It's a programming language in its own right. I spent many hours trying to understand what happened and how it happened. In the end, I wiped and rebuilt my own Windows 7 computer four times. Although I tried desperately to convince Bob that he was also infected, he did not believe it because nothing untoward happened. It is SO frustrating to have strange happenings and have no one believe you, even your own family. I feel this was done to make me feel unbalanced, distracted, and unsafe. That even my own computer is not safe. No computers are safe. They can disrupt our lives any time, and our computers, and we will never find the cause. **(**This is an important event that will be explained later)**.

4/3/18 11:17 PM one low-flying plane. Had a lot of entities in the bedroom last night. One touched my right foot and I respectfully demanded that Archangel Michael remove all entities not of love and light NOW!

4/5/18 A lot of entities in my room last night, I woke up at 5 AM. I had a dream about moving into different bodies and taking them over. Today I found a shirt that I just wore a little while ago in the bathroom on my counter. It had a bad smell, like B.O. or being in the laundry hamper but it's so strong that I can't wear it when it smells like this. I've had it happen before. I thought these smells were coming from the laundry room where the litter boxes are, so I've moved the shirts immediately into my closet. Imagine my surprise when I found these shirts had the same weird smell. Today I found two marks, one above each eye, as if I had needles in those areas. The "needle" marks are there and the skin around the marks is red and disturbed as it would be if needles (like thin acupuncture needles would leave a mark). So, this means I left my room—in my own BODY—physically. I'm wondering now if when I left last night or another night, I put on that shirt and when I came back, put it back on the counter and it smells because of the environment I was in. Also, when I saw these marks in the mirror I had an image of two needles and a wire between them and my own face. BASTARDS! I wonder what they are doing with me?! And I hope I can figure it out via clues.

4/6/18 My medium said the mark on my arm was from an IV. I have been noticing a lot that my clothing has a weird smell, like extreme B.O. or something. At first I thought I wasn't putting enough soap in the washer because I found clothes in the laundry room that had just been washed with this B.O. smell. Then, I thought it was the litter boxes and the clothing was somehow absorbing the smell of the litter boxes so I immediately moved the clothes out of that room. Then, I found clothes that I wore the day before had that smell and that's when I realized that I was leaving my house physically each night and those smelly clothes from the laundry room, my closet or those I left on the counter in the bathroom was what I wore when I left. If the clothes were folded in the laundry room, I must have folded them and put them back after coming back. I have also found clothes in the dryer that smell like this. These were clues. The medium said that I had been leaving for three days and coming back to the timeline when I left—in those clothes. I was noticing that my underarm hair was growing really fast and I needed to shave every day. The medium said to watch for other signs—like having grey hair after just having it dyed and I have to admit—I have seen this. I thought it was a bad or sloppy dye job. I will look for other clues now that I know what to look for. I am supposed to say "I AM THE SUN" to fry alien electronics.

4/7/18 One low-flying plane.

4/8/18 Woke up at 5 AM with something spasming in my body on the right side of my abdomen under my chest. I was lying on that side and it hurt a lot. I was told it was "organ turning."

4/8/18 Dream. Had multiple dreams about being in a classroom working with table seven on problems we were supposed to solve. I was late to class because my high-heeled white strappy shoes were filthy and I put foot, shoe, and all in the sink. But, I only did the right shoe, not the left. The left turned out to be dirty too.

4/18/18 Awake. Saw a guy in my bathroom and he looked like he was wearing a superman tight outfit (no cape). His head was squarish and looked like he was wearing a helmet. The person was there for one second and then was gone.

4/22/18 Woke up at 3:59 AM, not the usual 4:40 AM. My throat was dry and I thought I was getting a sore throat and I realized that while my throat was dry, my mouth was not. How is that possible?

4/24/18 Dream. Had a dream as I was waking up at 3 AM that five to seven beings in brown robes were standing in a group. They had red (crayon red) heads in the shape of an @ symbol, I woke up very cold.

5/1/18 Woke up at 4:30 AM extremely depressed like I'd never get back to remote viewing and that I wouldn't be able to solve my computer problems because I wasn't smart enough. This went on for about 15 – 30 minutes and I felt heavy and felt I should just give up on the computer and the remote access Trojan computer anyway. All of a sudden—I thought—wait a minute! I'm smart enough and I can figure this out. It's not hopeless and I thought—I'm smart and I have Bob to help me figure this out and the feeling lifted. I felt my vibration rise. This was a psychic attack.

5/1/18 Continued. I am working on remote viewing now and I will make sure I start on it immediately. Someone wants very badly for me to stay away from remote viewing—and they trashed my computer to make sure of it to either distract me or make me feel hopeless and unsafe.

5/3/18 Did a remote viewing. I listened to David Morehouse's practice session and instead of coordinates, I said I wanted to be invisible. I said I wanted to see who was looking at my computer. Because of the remote access Trojan, I was having extreme computer issues. I saw a former neighbor who hacked my computer, in an office building, in a big room—no windows. There was an angry looking guy looking at a computer. Suddenly, he turned and looked right at me! I freaked out and then remembered that I should have asked for protections before remote viewing. Yikes. Upon reflection, I'm not sure the "guy" was human. He had an angular face. His eyebrows made him look angry but he didn't look happy but very menacing. He probably wanted to scare me. I'll add the proper protections and do it again soon.

5/4/18 Woke up at 4:48 AM, a bit earlier. I felt like red lights were in my eyes. If I looked at it, I could go blind. I spent some time trying to make sure my eyes were closed but feeling like I was going to be blind. I rolled over and felt my pillow that I use for my back was dangerous and I kicked it off the bed.

5/15/18 Woke up at 3:37 AM screaming "There is something moving on the ceiling." I woke up Bob. I remember seeing black moving on the ceiling. I wonder now if this was a delayed reaction? Maybe this happened at the beginning of being taken and I was able to scream out when I was brought back at 3:37 AM? If I was brought back and taken at the same time, it makes sense.

5/15/18 Continued. I am leaving fingernail polish off my fingers. I will see if this makes a difference because my nails on my left hand have been altered. The polish is corroded off, damaged, peeled, chipped on a regular basis. Since I'm right handed, this is strange.

5/21/18 Last night I set out some specific clothes plus a note that said "where?" thinking that I would write on the note and say where I was going. Didn't happen.

5/21/18 Dream. Instead I had dreams of offices. Some were like movie sets of donut shops and people sitting around portraying different people. One dream was about a woman who went from a sterile white environment to a green environment where they had large candy vending machines that dispensed candy for free. This woman pushed some of the buttons and bunches of candy bars came out and I picked one that was chocolate mint with green nuts for breath.

5/21/18 Dream continued. In the donut shop, I was portraying a poor black man. Sometimes I was holding the poor black man. Sometimes I was him. He was being asked to make a choice but it was clear that they wanted him to make a specific choice. There really isn't a choice—it just seems like there are choices. The donut shop had desks, no tables. Like a classroom.

5/24/18 Felt sick all day and for several days had pain in my head and jaw. I tried **LaHoChi**—it helped a little. Found lumps on my head and a sore on my gum on the left upper gum. My tooth, bottom right molar was painful. No chewing on it. My head felt drilled with big lumps left behind. I tried out the seven layer prayer. It worked.

5/24/18 Continued. My medium wants me to say the following when I hear the ETs coming in: "I revoke all contracts" and "This is against my free will."

5/25/18 My medium wants me to try playing the "Triple Mantra" song by Nirinjan Kaur to help with ETs. I tried using binaural beats and **LaHoChi** under my pyramid. Got really hot.

5/25/18 Continued. Later I was thinking and realized that someone was in my head with me. I blocked them and I heard someone say, **"She blocked us, Sir."** It was strange that I could hear them.

5/26/18 The seven layer protection shields me from being psychically attacked and remote viewed. It does not protect me from being abducted. I was abducted last night. I remember being in a room with echoey floors. All I heard was the reverberating sound of someone walking in hard sole shoes across the loud floor.

5/26/18 Continued. Woke up and my right bottom molar hurt. I started up **LaHoChi** and asked that my tooth be healed and it feels fine now.

5/27/18 Came home from dancing at 1:17 AM. I started googling why aliens only come when you're asleep. I found www.themarsrecords.com on how to get rid of them. Metatech.org was another one. I realized that the noises I was hearing were remote viewers popping in. I heard the sounds (pulsing sounds) of a ship. I started to go to bed at 3 AM but decided to take a shower. In the shower I felt menaced, so I started grounding myself and respectfully demanding that the archangels get rid of the remote viewers and I did the seven layer protection prayer three times. While toweling off, I saw a picture in my head of me in my pyramid doing **LaHoChi** on myself. I asked, using discernment, yes three times if from God, Love and Light, and with my Christ Cloak of Truthfulness, heard a chorus of "Yesses" and ran to the pyramid. I used my bowls and banged on them to clear the space. I felt better but then heard the remote viewers all around me on one side of the room and then the other. I set my space then grounded myself, then did **LaHoChi**. My hands got really hot. Then, my spirit guides told me to do IET Angelic Healing on myself. I didn't know what to do, so I asked for guidance. There are no instructions that I know of to use IET on a person—on themselves. What they showed me was a pyramid shape on all of my chakras. So, I did that. I also used **LaHoChi** on my chakras asking for them to be cleared from energetic and physical obstacles. I also spent quite a lot of time removing implants via **LaHoChi**. After all of the healing in the pyramid, I heard a whistle outside. I had been begging for help from my spirit guides, Pleiadian Council of Light and Arcturian Counsel of Light and Koreg. After the whistling, I heard a bird, which I think was Koreg. I then noticed it was 5 AM and the sun was coming up. I went to sleep at 6:30 AM but I think they took me anyway and I realized that sunlight is not any safer than darkness.

5/27/18 Continued. I think this is part of my path. When it's happening to you, you are motivated to find what works and you are willing to do experiments because you have nothing to lose. During my healing session, I ran the Triple Mantra for extra protection. It can't hurt.

5/29/18 Remember dreaming about green and red lights as if I were looking at them from a foggy/raining/smudged window or a test tube. The tube glass was thick and hadn't been cleaned in a while or the glass was distorted and melting. As if the glass was moving/not set, like it was put there in layers and the layers were shifting.

5/31/18 Felt better today. Remote viewers were fewer last night. It sounded like little pebbles were hitting the windows. It sounded like one remote viewer got in, but there weren't a lot and there weren't a lot that got into my house. Maybe in general they were hitting a force field and that's the noise I was hearing. Woke up to that song "A Thousand Years" by Christina Perri.

6/1/18 Woke up at 5:30 AM with palms and inside forearms burning. Did **LaHoChi** to alleviate it. Had a dream about a family in my neighborhood. They were blaming me for something they did to me. My spirit guides told me it was a psychic attack. The dream had something to do with someone breaking into my "system." They had everyone against me and even had a small child informing me that they had no choice—they had people chasing me and tearing apart my house.

6/1/18 Continued. I heard the remote viewers last night. My clothes smelled again. So, I went somewhere but feel I am making progress anyway.

6/1/18 My medium thinks the remote viewers drove me to my pyramid to see what I would do and that's how they found out about my healing practice. This means they are NOT all knowing. Good info!

6/2/18 Discovered psychic attacks can be sent through the TV. I think my palms and inside forearms were burning to keep me from doing **LaHoChi** on myself. This must mean it works. I must continue!

6/5/18 Woke up and thought it was Friday, three days from now. I think I am abducted for three days and then returned.

6/6/18 Woke up at 5 AM. This must be when I come back. Last night at 12:34 AM or 0034, no one came. There were no remote viewers until 12:42 AM and 12:48 AM. My spirit guides say that a contract was broken and the remote viewers "terrorized" me and herded me into my pyramid on 5/28/18. I also woke up with a huge blister on my lower right jaw on my gum.

6/6/18 Continued. 1 PM Someone named Louise started talking to me today. She said she's the alter who goes into the ships and does the missions. She said Bob's alter goes by BoBo and he is in the military. Louise said "they" are concerned I'm figuring things out. I don't know who "they" are.

6/11/18 Got a lot of thoughts from someone else. I know that they are not mine whenever they are in a loop. I had to block them with a mirror shield. That way, they bounce off.

6/15/18 Was told I was a "frequency holder" by my spirit guides.

6/17/18 Asked my spirit guides for truth. Got it. Sometimes the truth is not all it's cracked up to be. Did a healing in the pyramid at 3 AM and heard popping. I demanded "SHOW YOURSELF" and then felt a chill. I think this means ghosts. I have to figure out how a RV feels vs. ghost or ERV or military remote viewer or other RV or entity. I will ask for guidance on helping distinguish between all of these entities.

6/17/18 Continued. Found a sore on the left top of my tongue. As if I bit my own tongue. I believe this may mean I'm still being abducted by someone. I regularly have gagging trigger events when I brush my teeth. Not every day but enough that I wonder where it is coming from. The only thing that makes sense is abduction. So, I think it is still happening. I'm going to figure out who it is and stop it.

6/17/18 Continued. Asked Ashtar Space Command to remove implants and to stop ET abductions.

6/18/18 I was at a movie today and tried out a few things like blocking the beam that comes out of the screen so that it would not affect anyone but the ETs were pretty angry that I was doing this. TVs and other screen have a beam of light or a specific tone that seems to affect people. As an experiment, I tried to block the signal from the screen for the movie goers. The ETs tried to distract me and when that didn't work, I found myself with a lot of headachy sore spots on my scalp and my left arm hurt. When I got home from the movies, I determined that the sore spots were implants, and I tried to clear them using everything I knew but it wasn't working. So, I asked my spirit guides for help with the removal of these implants. The implants moved under my fingers as I was trying to deactivate them. My spirit guides indicated to go to the pyramid, so I went there and called out for all medical teams to come out and help. It turned out that the implants were black metal octopi on my entire body but especially my head. Everything was hurting—my left arm, my back, head, sinuses, scalp, neck, etc. My spirit guides said this would take a while.

6/19/18 Woke up to sounds of typing. I felt like I was hooked up to something and someone was typing commands into a computer.

6/25/18 I finally understand how the ETs are able to use a loophole to obtain our permission to get us out of our beds. They THREATEN harm to our loved ones! This ensures compliance. This gets around free will. I'm going to use this against them.

6/25/18 Continued. I figured this out by thinking—why would I leave my bed each night willingly? They wipe my memory for multiple reasons—all self-serving. If I know their methods...I can fight them. If they know your fears...they can use them against you.

6/27/18 Had a dream about being in a hospital underground. I was in tunnels looking for people and it smelled down there. I was looking for a particular room. The walls were brown and dark and the ceilings were high as well as the doors. The doors were tall with frosted glass. I could see movement behind the doors. We, another person and I, were trying to avoid looking in.

6/27/18 Continued note to self: Try not to do giant healings outside of pyramid. Wait until you're stronger, otherwise big black octopi will come into you.

7/5/18 Felt awful all day with horrible headache and fatigue. Realized I needed to remove all energy suckers from the house. It all went away, after I did that. I guess I have to specifically ask that they be removed—the suckers. The wording of "all entities that are not in my highest and best good" is not good enough—not specific enough.

7/10/18 I need to say, "block any and all entities" not just "remove." Remove implies they are already in the space and allow them a loophole to return. Block is the word I need.

7/10/18 Continued. I blasted the implant in my own eye. It's gone. Archangels said that my healing muscle is getting stronger. The thing in my eye returned. I'll have to keep trying to get it out.

7/12/18 Figured out why I sometimes have marks like acupuncture on my forehead—it's because the ETs poke whatever is sticking out of the covers that they can poke with their compliance needles.

Why do ETs use needles? Maybe these are PEOPLE! I have these needle marks on the back of my head too. Bastards!

7/13/18 Home at midnight and I felt a compliance needle prick on my left arm. BASTARDS! I am not giving up. I will be doing some **LaHoChi** and Integrative Energetic Therapy Level 3 tonight. They poked me 10 times and when I blocked one ET, another would show up, poking me 10 times. I was blocking their needles. Progress. Since I was abducted last night I realized that the blanket ask of "please remove and block all ETs not in my highest and best good" was not working and I had to NAME the ETs specifically that I wanted to block. I asked the angels to help me figure it out.

7/13/18 Continued. Later, a friend came over and I gave her **LaHoChi** and Integrative Energetic Therapy. During our session I saw a big black octopus in her lungs. As soon as I started working on her lungs/heart, I started getting psychically attacked on my back. I then called in the Angelic medical team of my spirit guides to take over and get rid of this thing.

7/14/18 My right eye is transmitting! Someone is looking through my eyes.

7/15/18 My right eye would not turn off (it's very bright) and I tried various requests. I think it finally dimmed after I blocked all transmitting and receiving.

7/15/18 Continued. I must be careful NOT to say anything out loud that I don't want the ETs to know. Otherwise, I am safe. The ETs are not in our heads but they do listen and watch us.

7/15/18 Continued. Whenever I use **Integrative Energetic Therapy** for healing someone, I get interesting, fun dreams. Today I dreamed that Bob and I were in a hovercraft. It was like a tin can but with rounded edges that were thick. We flew around or hovered around. It was fun.

7/16/18 Dream. I had a dream that my phone got stolen. I was at a resort and remembered having it the night before but not today.

It was gone! The phone that was left as my phone was called ELANTRA in red letters. The phone was squat and a bit square and all of my stuff had been moved to the phone. All apps had red captions not white.

7/16/18 Continued. Did some ill-advised "healing" to try to stop mind control for the masses while at the movies. Then I had to sit in the pyramid asking for healing. Even after all of my healing in the pyramid, I still had some attacks happening. I'm reading a book on mind control and I'm still being attacked. That won't stop me. The book I'm reading is by Cathy O'Brien called *Access Denied*. The book also talks about a patented airwave way of mind control called The Sound of Silence. I was asking to block this and caused a shit storm to come my way. I was psychically attacked in the extreme.

7/17/18 I woke up at 3:30 AM and heard the words **"331, 331."** I suddenly realized that **331** was the time. I felt like I shouldn't move until **331** but I got out of bed to go to the bathroom and could not walk. I was off balance and stumbled around looking for my slippers (because I live in the desert and scorpions sometimes make their way inside). All I could remember was that there was an invisible fence around me until **331**.

7/17/18 Continued. I think this means I was abducted again. I don't know by whom. **331** must be a code word or maybe coordinates. I have woken up in this state before—feeling like I can't move (or shouldn't) because of some "rules." I hope it becomes clearer with time.

7/18/18 Discovered that the remote viewers are afraid that I will unlock something and are desperate for me not to RV. I will now make this a priority.

7/18/18 Continued. I am thinking of just listening to the CD for the remote viewers class that I got from the David Morehouse book and seeing what happens. What will be unlocked? I listened to the CD, did the exercises and got into a meditative state. I saw the colors. My left ear is now plugged.

7/19/18 Dream. Woke up at 3:40 AM. Had a vision/memory/dream and in it there was a very white-faced being like a man with black eyes. On one nostril someone placed a bunch of transparent insect wings—like six to eight total. The vision disappeared like a PowerPoint presentation slide visual animation where the picture becomes little squares and disappears.

7/19/18 Continued. I'm wondering now if the remote viewing will allow me to remember something. Whatever it is, they (the ETs or the government) want to keep it a secret.

7/20/18 Listened to the David Morehouse CD again and felt buzzing in my head.

7/21/18 While reading and watching TV at 6:30 PM, I saw a bright white light above the couch and it was rectangular. It was just a flash of this form and it was white.

7/23/18 Dream. Woke up at 4 AM with this recurring dream I have that I've forgotten to take my pills. This time I got more of a description out of the experience as I tried to figure out—what pills? The feeling was that I'm having issues because I continue to forget to take these pills. The pill in question is a pink pill and it's oblong. I already take a pink oblong pill each night and I have for years. This is the most info I've had on the "pills" I keep forgetting. The feeling is one of franticness and fear which leads me to believe that this is all ET based.

7/26/18 Learned that "Louise" uses my body in an abduction scenario. She is me, but I'm not her. My acupuncturist told me this.

7/27/18 I remembered hearing different tones in my ears. Some loud, some really loud, some soft, in both ears when I was sleeping.

7/28/18 Asked my spirit guides to help me lift the veils of illusion in my bedroom. I saw a white square, I saw a falling star, then two stars that flew up (as opposed to down). I saw two or more red eyeballs. I saw one red eyeball touch my right forearm between my elbow and wrist on the top. I saw a light green aurora borealis in the corner near my bed up high on my right side. I could not sleep until past 4 AM.

7/28/18 Continued. But, then I had a dream. I was standing with a man who could change his face into someone I knew. He was trying to draw me in. He was letting off this shower of spiraling fractals, like a curtain. They were like icicles raining down in an organized way from this head. They were clear, sparkling and spiraling. He tried to suck me into his sphere of influence. The only way out was to insult the person he was impersonating. I got away. The guy was pasty/chalky white. I don't remember his eyes.

7/29/18 Dream ELANTRA—I keep seeing this word in my dreams. ELANTRA—this word was at the top of a receipt that I received from a barista/coffee shop lady.

7/30/18 Woke up clutching the mattress heater controller for dear life. Thought it was a healing stone. I don't know what was going on there.

7/31/18 Dream. I was underground, dirt all around in a tunnel and I was working with people. There was a large man with his back to me. I went up to him to talk and said to him, "You look familiar." The man had teeth all over his face in clumps. He had greasy hair. It was gray and stringy and long. He was angry and grayish looking. He yelled at me to go away.

7/31/18 2nd Dream. A guy in a white shirt and dress pants told me that my invention would be reverse engineered if I left.

8/14/18 Whoever tortured me last night are not the same ETs as those with the needle like fingers. My throat hurt today when waking up = torture.

8/14/18 Continued. The mental block of blocking out all entities in your mind, not in the highest and best good only works for 24 hours. Lessons learned.

8/15/18 I turned on mind blocking today from 9 – 9 (12 hours). My clothes I put on today smell like lilac. I don't own anything that smells like lilac.

8/15/18 Continued. I was told that I am becoming who I am supposed to be. This does not mean I'm turning into a bug or something else. I will be becoming the me I am supposed to be.

8/15/18 Continued. During meditation I got this message: The ETs and government are afraid of your power. When you turn your brain off from their control, this scares them.

8/16/18 Could not sleep until 3:30 AM. Had a dream about the IDES of INS (Ides rhymes with tides) I was interviewing people asking them about the Ide's of Ins which was about dining with other people. I was speaking a different language and they were too and I could understand them.

8/16/18 Continued. I woke up with a gag reflex with my toothbrush in the front. This means I was tortured last night.

8/21/18 Dream. I had a dream where three guys came to abduct me. They were normal looking guys. One had a beard but they were surrounding me. One had a rectangular leather patch or leather piece—and that's what they were using to abduct me. I don't know what it was. It didn't create a stinging feeling—it just made me sleep.

8/25/18 Left the David Morehouse Facebook group today. A woman commented on my post from three months ago asking for help with blocking remote viewers. I blocked her, deleted my post and left the group. Her post gave me the willies and that's enough for me.

9/4/18 I was abducted by someone who placed a ":" in dots/needle/shot marks/bruises on my right upper arm. I do not know what this means. I am being abducted by different groups. I get rid of one and another takes its place.

9/11/18 Saw the acupuncturist today. He said I should use old Druid hieroglyphics instead of the newer "Egyptian" symbols. He gave me a printout and I've been looking at them but can't figure out what to do.

9/14/18 Saw a red eyeball at night as well as a yellow thing that looked like a gun of golden Christ light fired a golden Christ bullet and hit a FORCEFIELD and that was the result—like a splash of color when the bullet hit the force field around my bed. I also saw a round thing with yellow glowing dots and black dots. It was circular. I don't know what that was.

9/15/18 Heard about *Yoga Nidra*—an app—from some friends. Went out dancing and put a shield on. It was a weird night. I think all or most dancers are narcissists. Wow! It makes sense why I don't fit in there.

9/17/18 I feel a lot of things hitting me. It feels like embers from a fire hitting my arms. I ask if it's not in my highest and best good for it to be blocked and it stops and then comes back.

9/20/18 A neutral entity said they wanted to "talk" to me. I had to give my permission. I asked him/her what they would do in the same situation. I can hear them but not see them. I don't know their true agenda. They said, "That's a good question, I've never thought of that before." HMMM. I decided not to do it, too many unknowns.

9/21/18 Keep smelling something on my mail. It's on packages too. Kind of like an essential oil.

9/27/18 Woke up with a bruise on my left arm in the elbow crease. The bruise is near the vein. It wasn't there when I went to bed. I also woke up at 3:84 AM multiple times last night. (That is not a typo).

10/1/18 Woke up last night thinking I wasn't safe. There was an opening in the house—not a door—an opening. I puzzled that out for a while and was too scared to sleep. This must be from an abduction. Today I had gag reflex from my toothbrush, confirming my abduction and torture.

10/1/18 Continued. Had a dream where a friend got married to a guy named Joe Cummings and she changed her name to KQUEREN Cummings.

10/2/18 Dream. Had a dream about being in an auditorium with friends sitting around. When we went outside there was a large black ship in the sky. There were beige ships coming out of it, shooting at people. Bob was there and we knew what to do to shoot them down. Later, we were captured by the enemy and they wore black round helmets and had black skin. They asked us if we wanted a "shot" or not. I said, "NO!" A person got a shot and got bumps all over. The "enemy" looks like a pie, with a piece taken out of it, but that was the goggles. The skin was black and the body was human.

10/3/18 Woke up to seeing a green doorway with a "+ +" on each side. Had a dream someone had taken my right eye out and was squeezing it. It hurt.

10/7/18 Discovered that the cameras in the office—I have two ever since my computers were compromised, were offline while we were out to lunch, starting at 12:30 PM which is when we left. My computer is a lot slower now.

10/9/18 After going to bed last night a voice came into my room after I saw two bright orange lights hit the shield over my bed. This "man" was not from the light, not from love, not from god. He said, "You must honor your contracts." I said, "NO! I relinquish my contracts." He said, "then you will probably DIE." I said, "OK!" The "man" also asked, "Where are those computers?" I think he was talking about my two servers that I took out of the office months ago that were compromised. This guy was from a "20 and back" program. He claimed I was in a 20 and back program. A "20 and back program" is a black-budget program of the Department of Defense (DoD) where you work there for 20 years and when your

20 years are over, they regress you back to the age you were when you started working there.

10/10/18 Remote viewed what happened on my computer on 10/7/18 and I saw two heavily-armed guys or girls in green Army clothes walk through the front door and go to my computer and put something on it.

10/10/18 Continued. Later while driving in my car, I zoned out and found myself on another street, still driving! I think I was removed from my car and placed back by someone.

10/11/18 That thing is still in my eye. It's even brighter! Tonight in meditation, my spirit guides said that on 10/7/18 it wasn't my computers that were tampered with, it was the room itself and the ETs know I can remote view and didn't want me to see what they were doing. They put something in the room, like a tracker, so that when I go in there, a tracker attaches to me.

10/12/18 Discovered that the word "abduction" is a trigger word. This is about mind control and programming!

10/14/18 Last night before sleep a "neutral" remote viewer came back to ask about the computers again. I told him I didn't understand last time when he was asking about "contracts" that he was talking about a "20 and back contract" and I thought we were talking about soul contracts. I told him the computer issue with PowerShell was because a neighbor who hacked my computer put a USB drive on my computer and it spread and affected my entire network, including my computers and server. After my UPS and motherboard of our camera system was fried, I unplugged the servers for good and about one month ago, shut them down and removed both servers from the office. That was what the "20 and back" guy was looking for. Anyway, I outed the person who destroyed my computers and told the remote viewer that I thought she had used this PowerShell hack on tons of people including her neighbors in other cities because her husband was in the Air Force and they moved a lot. I think she was trying to frame me. I was told she would be taken care of, probably eliminated. I also asked if he could remove that program from my computer because it's undetectable.

10/15/18 Was meditating today and someone placed something on the back of my head, on the left side. It blocked me and I spent all night trying to unblock it. So, today I rewrote my "calling in Protections Each Night Manifesto" and used them because they call for "impenetrable fields." So, today, no remote viewers. I can hear them trying to get in and hitting the glass on the windows! HAHA! It was awesome!

10/16/18 It is 9:30 AM and I just heard a remote viewer. This means the impenetrable shield only lasts eight to nine hours. Not 24 hours. I will have to do this repeatedly, throughout the day.

10/18/18 Saw a red streak on the ceiling in the bedroom in morning with some sunlight in the room. Saw several shadows that moved quickly. So cool! This means, under the right conditions—dark enough and not too bright, I am seeing things with my eyes—not pictures in my head. Yay!

10/18/18 Continued. Last night there was a big firefight going on over my bed. The moving impenetrable shield around me expired and I felt it as I was driving home after meditation and there were beings in my car, possibly remote viewers and I was getting psychically attacked. 12 hours is the max.

10/17/18 In huge frustration trying to use my phone, someone was affecting my phone and causing the touch screen to have blank spots. I was texting to a friend when my screen wasn't working and in frustration I typed in "F**k off neighbor who hacked my computers." Then, I back spaced and erased it. This action fixed my phone! After remote viewing the situation, I think they pulled the plug on that person and they know I know who is screwing with my phone and I'm not afraid to out them. I think the importance is that I outed that person. When that guy was telling me that I had broken my contract and he was talking about a government contracts, not a soul contracts, I think he was talking about software I knew about or created in my government contract that this woman put on my computer. These things are related.

10/19/18 Dream. Had really long dream where I worked in a place that had very heavy air and it was hard to breathe. There was a dragon fly buzzing by at normal speed. Was this project called Project DRAGONFLY?

10/19/18 2nd Dream. The job I left behind was with servers. The guy didn't know how to run them and left me notes on paper asking questions. I felt bad but could not remember much about my last job but I didn't know why.

10/26/18 Dream. Had a dream and there was a person called LAFUZ in it.

10/27/18 Saw black rectangles, like I used to see years ago. I think this is my memory wipe. I remember trying to remember what this meant, which is: FEAR and LEARNING. I believe they are trigger words for the memory wipe and I will not be able to undo these in meditation. And it's interesting that "learning" is a trigger word. Is this to curb my great curiosity? I must find another word for each and work on those in *Yoga Nidra*.

10/27/18 Continued. I did experiments with my eye thing last night. I tried to get it to help me see the people controlling it, but instead someone talked to me—said his name was Deputy Colonel (?? Is this a real designation?) Dennis and he was with the Marines (US Marines). Also, I saw a big eyeball appear, near my bed. Then there was a big blue eye! The whole thing! Dennis said the US government was controlling the eye thing. Dennis passed my "highest good" test, BUT...the whole conversation was hinky. It was basically that I was in their program as a little girl and I am a natural remote viewer. My sister was in the program too but was not as smart and always angry and competing with me. This is true in real life. I also saw lots of lights, twinkling and a half-moon shaped yellow things. I saw lines of light and changes in lights in other parts of the room. It was as if something with some light was coming into the room.

10/28/18 KISSA KATHA KA— woke up with this word in my head.

10/31/18 This evening a thought about a woman who used to be interested in Bob popped into my head. I said out loud, "I'm not afraid of losing Bob," and the thoughts left my head. It was as if someone was standing beside me, manipulating my thoughts and when I made that comment, that person left the room. Powerful! This was HUGE! How many thoughts actually originate from ME? How many thoughts originate from elsewhere? I will be saying, "I am not afraid," to all thoughts until I can figure out which ones are my true thoughts.

11/2/18 Woke up at 2 AM hearing another language in my ear. It wasn't Spanish—it was nothing I had ever heard before.

11/4/18 Discovered that the cameras in the house were off the week of 10/27-11/3 (when I was out of town) because there were people in our office. They left a cabinet door above my monitor open and my UPS on the floor beside my computer was pulled away at an angle from my computer. I am so angry! I also could not remote view the situation. They were blocking me.

11/5/18 I was finally able to remote view what happened in my office while I was gone. They went to my computer and used some kind of equipment to test my hard drives. I had unplugged power to my hard drive and in addition, had unplugged the Ethernet cable because I did not want to have to reinstall another Windows drive. Anyway, the people used equipment to take off the software on it and all drives on my computer. I never removed the other hosed drives. They went to my server in a closet and used that equipment on there as well to remove the software.

11/8/18 Realized yesterday that powerful beams of negativity are coming from TVs, so I added a transmutation to love and light and sent it back.

11/10/18 Last night I felt menaced in the room and put up some protections. They worked, for now.

11/10/18 Continued I found a new implant in my right eye. It was striped! But there is also an implant in my left eye now. I hope I can get rid of it.

11/11/18 On the way to dancing last night I had a very weird experience. I was daydreaming that I was in an interview for an IT position and was being ask about an old job at a now defunct Department of Defense (DoD) company. I was being asked why I left. I said, "new opportunities." Then the interviewer asked about two specific people I worked with (two chuckleheads) and I got the impression that the interviewer knew them or expected me to work with them. So, I said, "Yes I worked with both of them." I didn't want to say anything bad about them but it morphed into me telling the interviewer that one of the guys was an incompetent boob and he wanted another incompetent boob to be my boss and that's why I left. **This morphed into me realizing that the "interview" was real and the interviewer was telling me that they wanted me back in a "20 and back" program.** I said "NO!" I don't want to do it anymore and then they said, "But you're on Sysadmin," on Reddit, meaning I subscribed to Sysadmin, which is true and I said—"they're my people." Then, he said, "So and so said he liked working with you," and I said, "I did what so and so told me to do plus so and so knows more than I do about IT." Finally they said, "We need you to come back," and I said, "NO! It's against my free will. I will not. I don't do it anymore." Blocking didn't work and I could still hear them talking about me—in my own head. Why now? What's strange is that this interview shit just popped into my head like a "normal" daydream but it was like a remote view. I saw myself in the interview—saw my facial expressions. I was watching myself and then it changed into a back and forth conversation that I was having in my head with someone! This incident had a dream like quality.

11/11/18 Continued. They also spoke to me about unplugging my computer before I left for vacation. They said something like: "Why did you unplug the hard drives before you left?" So, I said, "I didn't want anything to be placed on my computer like last time. That last time I was unaware that I had to worry about such a thing and I wanted to make sure if anyone used a computer illiterate again, it wouldn't be easy. The computer illiterate would have to work at it and it would take longer. The computer illiterate would need some know how. Take off the cover, etc. I didn't want any more stuff on my computer." The he said something like, "Why didn't you just take it off? You created it." I said, "I don't remember anything and had no idea how to take it off."

11/14/18 Woke up thinking I had just taken a drink of slimy water. This must be the reason for my aversion to toothpaste in my mouth and it dripping out. This makes me gag.

11/15/18 Last night I did a future remote view to see how the ETs get me out of my bed at night. They use tones of some type that are in my subconscious and I get up and put clothes on. Then we walk out the windows and into a little ship. They come in through the window.

11/15/18 Continued. Last night, I left the living room and went into the bedroom to read. After a while of not facing the TV, I felt attracted to some books I had gotten a while back written by Stewart A. Swerdlow. They make more sense to me now. Last night I did some exercises from these books and added a violet tetrahedron. I will make this a part of my regular healing practices.

11/15/18 Continued. Change of scenery can mean a different room, not facing TV. TV is used for programming of the masses.

11/17/18 Listened to some sacred angelic soul sounds. I felt different. I hope it helps.

11/18/18 Woke up saying "Yaaaaaweeeeeeeh," over and over. This must be something important. I then heard someone say, "Enough!" I can feel my vibration raise when I say this word.

11/20/18 Dream. Had a dream that the sky was spinning and we could see ships in it. LOTS of ships. (No gravity.) The sky was moving in circles.

11/21/18 Remote view. Using the book, *The Hyperspace Helper: A User-Friendly Guide,* by Stewart A. Swerdlow and Janet D. Swerdlow, I was trying to look at a scrape on my right index knuckle. The scrape appeared this morning. I saw a pointy faced human who put me in a cage underground. I was there because I wouldn't cooperate. They called me feisty. Said I have many gifts and I would not use them for this guy/people. I rolled the cage a few times and got the scrape. The guy looks like the same guy that I remote viewed in the windowless room that looked straight at me and scared me one of the first times I was remote viewing. I asked why my "people" allowed me to be taken. I was told that my higher self allowed it—part of my experience. I don't believe that for a minute. Liars!

11/24/18 On vacation. I brought my book *The Hyperspace Helper: A User Friendly Guide*. But, tonight I asked my higher self to "show me" and saw two standing alligators!

11/25/18 After using the "**Communication Archetype**" from the book *Healing Archetypes & Symbols*, I had great success communicating with Bob a lot better. I had him use it tonight and we'll see if we can communicate even better. When I needed to communicate with him, I was articulate, instead of not being able to find the correct word. Later, when he couldn't hear me, instead of getting mad and yelling, I simply turned my head towards him. It was GREAT!

11/25/18 Continued. Today I was feeling like a negative Nelly and decided to raise my vibration. As I did this, I felt something LIFT OFF my body. Something was attached to me, making me feel this way. Amazing discovery.

11/25/18 Continued. I am cancelling out things (1) Intruders taking me out of bed against my free will (2) psychic attacks (3) pointy things around me (4) programming. I might as well give it a shot and see if I can get rid of it this way.

11/26/18 I have felt for a very long time that the space protections do not work. Maybe they work for some things. It is unclear what they do or don't do. Instead, I'm using "**Ultimate Protection**" from *The Hyperspace Helper*. This protection works! As an experiment, I didn't do my setting sacred space protection last night, but I did put a mirror bubble around me and I cancelled out any standing alligators/intruders.

11/26/18 Continued. I had no dreams/don't remember any but I also don't remember any black rectangles which means memory erasing. I don't know what this means. More data is needed.

11/26/18 Continued. We found out that our garage door opened while we were at home on 11/24/18 at 7 AM Bob has an app on his phone that watches the garage door and notifies him if it opens or closes. The app DID NOT work! I am going to remote view this situation to see who and what was going on. I placed my entire house under the "Ultimate Protection" so it will be interesting to see what/who did this. Last time we were away, our cameras inside our house did not function. This time it was the garage door app.

11/27/18 Today I did a remote view with a memory of waking up screaming when I lived with my first husband in 1986. I could not see anything except orange and red. I'll keep trying. The black rectangle was present indicating a memory wipe. It was clearly horrifying and that's why I can't remember or see it.

11/27/18 Continued. I asked my oversoul—why are they watching me so closely? The answer: "They know your worth."

11/27/18 Continued. I started remote viewing exercises and I saw myself in my bedroom at home when I first got the Swerdlows' books. Two entities were standing on either side of me, putting a stick or baton to my head on each temple. I stopped reading the book because it felt too esoteric. Two pointy faced guys are using the batons. They left, like in a spiral. They went underground and said, "That'll stop her for now." I asked why can I see this now and why did I feel attracted to these books now? I was told "more protections against them are in place now." I also saw a big ship over my house and the sky is filled with ships. They are trying to block out the sun—but I can see through. I was told, "for now you can."

11/28/18 Tried to cancel out broad categories like: cancel out all entities, all entities that lead me out of bed at night, all entities involving tones in ears, certain people, narcissists, any entities I can't see, memory wipers, torturers, etc. Found a big scratch on my right buttock. It was swollen and painful.

11/29/18 Last night two bright white flashes were in the room of our hotel. Bob even saw it. My spirit guides even told me it was "them" because electronic devices do not work properly when they are in the room.

11/29/18 Continued. I am seeing things out of the corner of my eye in daylight now. I haven't figured out what I'm seeing yet, but I will.

11/29/18 Continued. Did another remote view of 1986 with first husband. What I saw was this: Two little beings take me and both are holding one hand and we walk through the wall/window, like it's a big sheet of fabric. We are now in a ship, operating table with bright lights. I can't move or speak. It hurts! I am prodded and they take my eggs. I burn. I feel uncomfortable like I'm in a gynecological exam. They are touching me and examining me. I can't believe this is happening to me again. I am there for what seems like several days. Finally, I wake up in my own bed. I remember the rectangle and start screaming. The black rectangle = FEAR.

12/6/18 I've learned that using Ultimate Protection blocks everything—the good, the bad, the ugly. But—it turned off my immune system protection and it allowed me to get a virus, that went to my chest so I did not renew it today.

12/6/18 Continued Today I found bruises on my left knee and thigh (on the outside of the leg)—6 FINGERS! They hurt. I found a bruise on my right knee with three dots on it—or needle marks. The thigh marks look like a crooked T. So, I don't know if it's a handprint or what it is. They held onto me tightly though. I had these bruises yesterday too. While my thigh hurt yesterday, there were no marks. My knee had one needle mark yesterday and today I have three needle marks!

12/6/18 Remote view. Did a remote view of these bruises and saw the following: An angry man said, "She's fighting us! If she wants a fight, we'll show her a fight. Who does she think she is? We decide what happens to her, not her." The man wasn't anyone I recognized, then he held me down and put what looked like a caulking gun up to my skin. "That should fix her."

12/6/18 Continued. I think I'm considered a slave. I cancelled out anyone who thought of me as a slave.

12/8/18 There is something in my left eye too!

12/9/18 Cancelled out any being that installed implants and any that feel that they own me.

12/10/18 Was told there was a beam coming from the TV when it was turned on.

12/10/18 Continued. I did not wake up in the middle of the night hot. I used to think it was a hot flash but it's a BEAM.

12/10/18 Continued. Found out that when my arm hurts during a healing, even my own, it's someone directing pain to my arm. When I blocked it, the pain stopped.

12/10/18 Continued. Did some **LaHoChi** stacking where you add people, three at first and more later, to your own self-healing.

12/11/18 Cancelled out all entities who made indentation or drill holes or sores on my scalp/skull. I regularly find indentations and bruises, painful spots on my scalp/head.

12/11/18 Continued. My spirit guides said that "the bad guys" are being more careful now that I'm cancelling them. Before when they thought they had all the power and technology, the flaunted their toys and techniques. Now that they know I'm using the information to systematically cancel everything, they are being more careful. They are using all manners of dirty tricks and technology.

12/11/18 Continued. This morning I woke up at 4 AM without feeling uncomfortably hot. This morning at 11 AM, however, I woke up hot.

12/12/18 I'm not sure if the cancelling out is permanent or semi-permanent or if loopholes are found that negate them. That's why some are repeated. I do this as needed.

12/12/18 Continued. Nothing would turn off my eyes. No amount of cancellation touched them. Sometimes the words I used shut down the right eye, but it came back on but not as bright.

12/12/18 Continued. Found something under Bob's cup holder in the couch that made his glass vibrate with certain tones. I recorded it. Bob couldn't hear it until I recorded it. It's still there and disguised as noises that sparkling water bubbles make but it sounds to me like ticking. Like tinny-sounding ticking.

12/12/18 Dream. On some sort of ship. I was in a strange cafeteria where food popped out of this machine—hot—but sometimes stuff you didn't order came with it. I got one piece of gum in an accordion pack, some potato salad that I was mad about and wanted to throw back at the guy, a pickle that was hollowed out and brown (like cola brown). Yuck. After eating there was a level above the eating area where you used a hose to breathe something in and you would rise up to the next level to play.

12/12/18 Remote view of the last couple of nights when I got bruises on my skull in the back, indentations, and sore spots. Taken and dragged out of bed by military in green. Taken to facility. Doctors place a machine on my head (like a narrow coffee can with two knobs on the flat part) and try to suck something out. The doctors say that they do what they are told and "they" are looking for something. One person says, "Look at her head! Jesus! How many times has this been done?" "Too many," says the other. Saw a black figure outside the window facing me—I was on the couch facing the window. It was holding something I couldn't see it—like a hose. The figure looked like a praying mantis but with glasses on.

12/14/18 Today I woke up with a pus bubble on my gum where I had a tooth extraction. I put my breakfast (cream of wheat) in the microwave and then was taken somewhere—in an instant—brought back to discover (1) bubble on gum was gone (2) microwave had 1:30 (1 minute 30 seconds) and it was still on 1:30—it hadn't moved. It wasn't counting down—the noise was there but no cooking. STRANGE!

12/14/18 Continued. My clothes still have the B.O./feet smell but only those put in laundry room and folded. I am still being taken. I will cancel out and see if I can get this to stop.

12/14/18 Remote view of who was making my head hurt yesterday? Same group as in the window on 12/12/18. PEOPLE! Two men. They were wearing black masks and using a big hose. The hose was spewing black smoke (dust onto my 3rd eye and my crown). There was a big ship over the house. The hose came from a ship and they were concentrating on my head—the top of my head. White light was beating the black stuff off. When I raised my hands to my 3rd eye to make the triangle with my fingers—they both gasped and jumped back and yanked on the hose to leave.

12/15/18 This evening my 3rd eye was hurting and as I faced the window in the family room, I activated LaHoChi and asked to block the BEAM hitting me from wherever it was coming from. My head stopped hurting. Yay!

12/16/18 Woke up with two needle marks. One was on my left wrist where I wear my watch and the 2nd one was on my left thigh, on the top. The wrist one kind of looks like a mosquito bite. The thigh one is definitely a big dark bruise with a NEEDLE mark in the middle.

12/16/18 Dream. Saw a photo of flowers on plants. The colors changed—turquoise, lavender, and coral. It looked like it was in water. I recognized that this was happening and I was dreaming the same thing over and over.

12/16/18 Continued. I keep hearing someone talking in my head and saying, "She calls us ASSHATS!" and then another person saying, "She doesn't know who we are—of course she lumps us all together." I can't tell who they are if they can hear me or if this is a current conversation.

12/16/18 Continued. Why would PEOPLE in weird outfits/gas masks pump something into my house? Into my 3rd eye? Into my right shoulder blade in the back? Why? Why? Why? I have to know the truth! Clearly there are asshats and others. I can't tell who is who. Or maybe this is a trick to make me THINK they are not all asshats!

12/16/18 Remote view. I saw that I was in a medical facility. They were hurting me. My eyes were out of my head. They were using that machine on my head (the coffee can with buttons—but this time there were four buttons). I was screaming and crying "MOMMY, DADDY! MOMMY! DADDY! It hurts, it hurts, stop, stop!" My legs/feet were in stirrups—like a gynecological exam. I was a little girl. My dad was in another room and they were telling him he agreed to this—as a soldier. He doesn't believe this and gets mad. He walks by the "operating" room and cries out: "OH MY GOD!!"

12/16/18 2nd Remote view of why do people take me each night, who are they and what they do. Army men. First they stuck me in the wrist, then the thigh. I went on a ship (spaceship). They said, "She blasted out the teeth implants," and they were putting it back. Then the tooth extraction spot—I thought it was a pus filled blister—it was an implant coming out. So, they took me while I was on the phone talking to the dentist and took it out. This changed how the microwave worked and that's why it was still stuck on 1:30 and that's why the "pus blister" was gone. Each time I blast something out, they put it back. I am programmed for some reason and they are watching me because everyone else wants me. They talked about how I keep going and this is part of my programming. I was there for a week while they put the implants back in.

12/17/18 Woke up multiple times last night. Woke up at 3 AM, 3:30 AM, 3:38 AM and each time I woke up I felt differently.

12/17/18 Continued. 3:00 AM—ABJECT TERROR—pushed out all other things. I was in BED. So, I thought, what about LOVE? Woke up at 3:35 AM, felt "normal"—loved and SAFE. Woke up at 3:38 AM—TERROR!

12/17/18 Continued. The terror feeling was huge and oppressive. It was hard to think of anything else. Cold, hard, trapped, voice of anything else, stark, aloneness. Was this a program? TERROR & NORMAL? In the car today whenever I saw the sun glinting on the cars in front of me, there was this pattern of dots that I saw each time I closed either eye. It finally went away.

12/18/18 So, last night I hear a voice in my head say this:

"THEY HAVE CROSSED THE LINE. YOU HAVE BEEN GIVEN A FREE PASS!"

ME: WHO IS THEY?

THEM: (no answer)

ME: WHAT DOES FREE PASS MEAN?

THEM: (no answer)

ME: I DON'T KNOW WHAT FREE PASS MEANS.

THEM: YOU WILL.

12/18/18 Continued. None of my guides or oversoul or anyone would tell me what this meant. So, I went to my medium and she said my free pass is NO KARMA for something I did and "they" fractured and obliterated two of my aspects that were made into glass. Or, that's what I got out of it anyway. The dots in my eyes and TERROR are related. It was from a long needle piercing my eyes. And the LOVE I felt in between the TERROR was fake—meant to feel like LOVE.

12/18/18 Continued. My medium says that I need to stop what I'm doing and go back to basics and I'm setting my sacred space wrong.

12/18/18 Continued. While driving in my car, I had a thought come into my head about the two chuckleheads I used to work with at that same DoD company and then my thoughts were hijacked by an ASSHAT asking me about working with these same chuckleheads. **I realized then that they were in my head and this was real.** I told "him" that I had chosen my spiritual path and I was not going to give away any more of my life. AND, I reminded him that I knew what they did to me as a little girl and I reminded them that I saw a scene where they had taken my eyes out AND did unthinkable harm and pain to my uterus or nether regions. And, it was against my free will and whatever they promised me—I'm sure they didn't deliver and I don't trust them. They then told me they would "get" Bob and I said he was on his own journey. They threatened me! but, I'm not doing it and I don't care what it is! Then, I blocked them.

12/19/18 I told Bob no emotional blackmail. If he is approached to work for the feds or the Secret Space Program, and the way they try to make him work for them is by threatening ME, to say "go ahead, this is her journey." This is my choice. I told him already I didn't allow any emotional blackmail on him when they threatened to do something to him, I told them, "go ahead he has his own journey."

12/19/18 Continued. My real life is my fake life and my dream/nighttime life is real life. It sucks and is depressing.

12/20/18 Woke up at 1:11 AM and couldn't see out of either eye—very blurry. I had a bump near my right eye where the ASSHATS did something to the right eye—it affected both. Couldn't read anything—not even the artificial tears wrapper. Finally able to make out that I had the artificial tears and opened it and placed some in both eyes. NOTHING HAPPENED! The eyes appeared to have a greasy smudge on them—it was blurry and greasy looking. Went back to bed to wrap my head around this possible permanent condition—no driving—no dancing—different life. Then, I got up and realized that there were NO SOUNDS. It was EERILY quiet. I couldn't hear Bob breathing. No kitties snoring. No angels. I was blocked. I could feel NO ONE, hear NOTHING. Archangel Michael could not hear me and I did not know what to ask for—except healing. My eyes were not getting better. Then I decided to chant **YAHWEH**. While chanting **YAHWEH**, the eyes started to get clearer and CLEARER. Suddenly, I wasn't blocked. I saw colors, yellow, green, and I continued chanting and at 2:44 AM, eyes returned to NORMAL. Then I felt two asshats poking me with their "sleep aid needles." I chanted Yahweh and only felt safe while I chanted. I then asked Archangel Michael to help me construct speakers around my body continually chanting YAHWEH. Then, I feel asleep. I was also chanting YAHWEH TUUU TEE. I think this is important.

12/20/18 Continued. I think YAHWEH is an important healing tool. Maybe multipurpose. YAHWEH TU TEE—extra potent? Unsure at this point. Maybe this "tone" stops the abductions? Definitely deprograms something.

12/20/18 Cancelled out all who affected my eyes negatively. BASTARDS!

12/20/18 Continued. Had the realization that the emotional blackmail is a catch 22. There are NO choices. I never had a choice in the Secret Space Program and Dad didn't have a choice. They want you to think YOU made a choice. You didn't. It's all fake. They are liars.

12/20/18 Continued. I am on the right track here.

12/21/18 Made realization that nanites are being pumped into the house by the guys with the gas masks. I cancelled these out and asked Bob to do the same. He did it. The nanite realization came to me because (1) my packages/mail has their weird smell, (2) my scissors in the drawer had the smell, (3) silverware straight from the dishwasher has the smell and (4) my sink has something growing on it in the master bathroom but not Bob's sink! It's something artificial and it looks black but it's not mold. Cancelled out all nanites.

12/22/18 Smelled my sweater from last night and it smelled like peppermint. This is different than normal. I have decided to hang up my clothes that I don't want being used off world. Otherwise, I take them (under ET programming) and use them and fold them back up.

12/22/18 Continued. ETs/abductors are all narcissists and this means: liars of everything. They use what you say against you. Don't tell them anything.

12/22/18 Continued. My recording of my medium's session doesn't work—I can't transcribe it and I think my computer is compromised, as well as my phone. Just the recording of 12/18/18 doesn't work—everything else works.

12/23/18 Did a healing on a friend, she saw a Reptilian eyeball during her healing. She even described it as that.

12/24/18 Woke up with a mark near my right eye. I also woke up with the left side of my neck sore and left shoulder.

12/24/18 Continued. This Ultimate Protection does allow some "entities, people, remote viewers, and ETs" to get in. I had to change who I block.

12/24/18 Continued. I'm figuring out that the Praying Mantis = 1 group, the military = 1 group and the Secret Space Program = 1 group. I do not know if these groups overlap. Today, I almost went to the bathroom, on auto pilot. I did not have to go. Caught it just in time. Was this my programming?

12/25/18 Three dreams—fragments: (1) Had a piece of paper between my thumbs. It was black with circuitry on it. One thumb caused a blue circuitry on the left to light up. The other thumb (right) caused a red circuitry to light up. (2) Was asking for help and was told a woman could help me. She wrote the word "PRINCE" in quotes. This person referred to me as a guy. So, I was a man in this dream. And (3) Black (Spy vs. Spy) face. The mouth was red, orange, and yellow.

12/25/18 Continued. I think the hierarchy of ETs is: Grays, Draco, Praying Mantis and "entity/being." Not sure who or what that is. No one cared when I cancelled out the Grays, Draco's, or Military but when I cancelled out the Praying Mantis—THIS is when I felt the TERROR/FEAR arise—INTENSELY. The Praying Mantis must be near the top of the being's hierarchy. The praying mantis creature usually pokes me with needles to sleep as well as thwap me on the lady parts.

12/27/18 Someone who said they were from ASHTAR Space Command started talking to me and suddenly I started sensing entities in my room—POKING me with needles and making LOUD noises. Being unsure who it was, I respectfully demanded that Archangel Michael remove them. Some stayed and more came and there were more needle pricks. So, I did some **YAHWEH** and they ALL disappeared and the room cleared and felt warm and calm.

12/28/18 Used YAHWEH each time I heard a THUNK or POP. I said this silently. It works!

12/28/18 Continued. Five people sent me their thoughts last night and I had a hard time blocking them.

12/28/18 Continued. I fell asleep at 3 AM and woke up at 4 AM. It felt like I had been asleep for two days.

12/28/18 Continued. There was some guy from the NSA in my head all day. The only way to get rid of him was to say **YAHWEH**. The lesson is: don't let your guard down. Don't trust anyone.

12/29/18 I am YAHWEHING every noise I hear. To do meditation, I clear the room with my singing bowl and saying YAHWEH... it was magical! Everything left. Yay me!

12/30/18 Woke up scared at 2:19 AM (Not petrified). Could not remember the dream. Each time I woke up scared, I said Yahweh. This means that Ultimate Protection does not work on all beings, but Yahweh does.

12/30/18 Continued. Had a dream about being given a box of computer parts and parts that didn't belong. I built my own computer and using my Windows 7 license, I had a new working computer. I have no idea if I was tricked by the asshats into taking a computer job!

12/30/18 Continued. Went to Angel Message night tonight. Got a message that the playing field is being leveled. I must be doing something right.

Chapter 32
My Experiences
2019

1/2/19 I am right about narcissists. They rule the Earth. They are everywhere, making our lives miserable.

1/3/19 Decided to teach a class on the Swerdlows' books on January 5, 2019 with some friends who I think can use it and spread this info.

1/4/19 Couldn't sleep until 3:30 AM but I woke up at 4 AM with an image of Shaggy—the man who I see all the time in my remote views; long hair, aviator glasses, and beard wearing a white coat. I cancelled him, in my dream. Not when I woke up—DURING.

1/4/19 Continued. I am blasting the nanites with EMP. I think it's working.

1/4/19 Continued. I just realized I have leveled my own playing field!

1/4/19 Continued. I had another idea about asking Mr. Swerdlow for reprints of certain pages and then go to UFO support group and share when I know/learned to level the playing field for others.

1/4/19 Continued. My spirit guides wanted me to know that my medium did not have the answers I needed and I had to find them and experiment. My medium wanted to place blame/victimization and wanted me to do the same mantra—Love, love, love which we need but we need BOTH TOOLS! This is the power. I knew it wasn't working or wasn't enough and she thought I wasn't trying hard enough. My guides say that my medium needed to know (for growth) that working together is the key. Not one person has all the answers and the other listens. This is UNITY!

1/4/19 Continued. I'm wondering if I should do the Ultimate Protection every two days instead of three.

1/4/19 Continued. Saw a quiet black blob shadow. It tried to keep to the shadows but I was able to see it. It didn't make any noises. I cancelled it.

1/5/19 I had my class on Swerdlows' books today. It was a lot for my friend who saw a Reptilian eyeball during a healing I was doing on her. But, I was told I had to bring her up to speed.

1/5/19 Continued. I cancelled out all technology.....and some other stuff, and the pain in my back went away. I did this specific wording because cancelling out BEAMS did not produce any results. I have to do experiments with my wording. I must be systematic, methodical, and precise with my cancellation wording.

1/6/19 How do the people, AI, hybrids, etc., get me to leave my bed? How? Why? What is the real agenda? I'm starting to think this is a distraction. A smoke screen.

1/6/19 Remote view of the guy I cancelled out while dreaming. Shaggy was a doctor. He pretended to be my friend. I cried before I was put under. He and seven other doctors gave me brain surgery as well as surgery on my abdomen (or lady parts) unclear. The operating room was green and everyone wore green scrubs with white masks and white gloves. My dad watched through the window and started screaming at them. They rushed over at the door.

1/6/19 2nd Remote view. Shaggy "found" me and "cultivated" me. I didn't like him. He hurt me. At some point he was kicked out of my care. A higher up doctor and an alien took over. The alien was gray, and tall with pointy features. He kind of looked like a stork. His arms were like fins. He took over my care. They aged me to 12 and held me. I was guarded my military men. I was 12 when I started my period which they monkeyed with. Each time an egg was produced, they took them until no more eggs would come out. My body only had so many eggs and they took them all. They took my DNA and eggs to make clones. The Grays (the littles) worked for him. I was "special" and smart. They tried to make smart clones of me. When they were done, they age regressed me to seven years old.

1/6/19 Continued. Found nanites in my sugar. The sugar in my tin, has what feels like rocks in it. I opened a new bag and no rocks, until the next day, then rocks. So, I bought some sugar packets, because I'm not eating those things. I EMPed all sugar in my house. It helps a lot but not enough, so I'll be eating sugar packets when I need them, not opened sugar.

1/6/19 3rd Remote view to see who takes me and how. Army guys in dark green uniforms with guns get me out of bed. We go through a wall to another doorway to another location. We go to a place where all of my selves and aspects work—one is a programmer, one is a pilot, one works on Mars. We work for the aliens—the tall gray alien. He sits on a throne. I was harmed because I was setting an example for the others not to rebel. I rebel. The aliens that own the Earth are looking for something, a key for humanity. They can't find it. Humans work for him. The dark green army guys wear dark green ball caps and they carry black or green guns. They have special ancient technology that allows them to FREEZE the people protecting me. And their ancient technology allows them to circumvent the Ultimate Protection.

1/7/19 Had no dreams but I did had a period of fear.

1/7/19 Continued. I just heard someone in my head telling me he hacked my higher self. I cancelled him. He's gone now. I think he was trying to intimidate me.

1/7/19 Continued. I'm starting to see purple swirls with gold on the outside. The gold sparkles and then disappears.

1/8/19 I will teach another class on Swerdlows' tools on February 10, 2019 at my house.

1/8/19 Dream. I had a dream that someone should start printing 3D car parts—especially for hard to find car parts.

1/9/19 I keep finding that my cuticles have been irritated. Every morning, another finger on either side (inside or outside cuticle) is irritated and hurts. What in the HELL are they doing?

1/9/19 Continued. I think memories and dreams are the same.

1/9/19 Remote view on what I need more information on: Operating room scene with large gray being. Multiple doctors— some are other Grays. Dad sees them all. He cries. He sees my eyes on the table and my head all bloody from the drilling. They have opened me up, slit me down the middle. The "boss" thinks that because of the shape of my toes, I "might" be the "one." The next day I will be made older so that I can have my eggs harvested. They put me back together and use a "pen" of sorts to hide the surgery lines. No one will be able to tell, but the marks on my skull stay because they think hair will cover it.

1/9/19 Continued. While writing this remote view down in my notebook, I can see an eyeball on my right hand between the webbing on the thumb and where my pen rests. Is this a remote viewer? The eye is BROWN. Human?

1/9/19 2nd Remote view. I went down a brown corridor to a room with double shiny steel doors with portal windows. The doors open when you push them with your body. It is institution green inside the room. This is all I see. The floors are light chocolate brown and are concrete—shiny concrete.

1/10/19 Had a dream where a friend sent me a wall of text in yellow with book titles. I remote viewed this dream and I could see one of the titles. It was *Thinking: How the Brain Works.*

1/10/19 Remote view. Down the corridor of brown to the green operating room with the portal windows and shiny metal doors, the operating room was institutional green. There was a huge gallery above. It was packed with people. I was on the table and a big silver machine was on the ceiling. I was naked and the machine covered my stomach. My eggs were aged so that they could be harvested. The machine was silver and it didn't touch me. Somehow the eggs were sucked out. The doctors were Tall Grays and other humans. Humans and Grays watched the surgery.

1/10/19 2nd Remote view. Children talking. I'm there with several others. We are prisoners and being held as "science experiments." We were grouped by having the same types of toes. The doctor reported our toes and that's how they found us. We are a group (of people I know in real life). We won't know each other later. There are babies there. We heard them.

1/10/19 3rd Remote view. The parents are required to bring their babies and hand them over. The babies can't talk or remember. The surgeries on us burn for a little while but don't hurt later. We are in a dormitory with single beds and thin mattresses. Everything is brown. The bedding, blanket, metal on the beds. The room is brown—a dark brown. We try to memorize each other's names so that we will remember them later. Besides science experiments, we don't know why we're there. We talked about them watching and listening to us all the time.

1/11/19 Woke up at 4:03 AM with the vision of a man (human) with a beard, shaggy hair—reddish-brown and two pairs of tiny glasses, one worn over the other. The glasses were black or purple. He was sucking something out of my head—like energy. I could feel it—just in my head. I woke up cancelling out that guy.

1/11/19 Continued. Fell asleep around 8 AM and dreamt about a human holding a silver tube—like a gun. I couldn't see the whole thing but I could see the hairy arm holding it. It was a white human arm. The man told me that I "skootch down in bed" to get away from it because the "shots in the butt hurt really bad." I think the shots in the butt are what are hurting my back every day.

1/11/19 Continued. I was told that humans using alien technology are at the heart of this—not just ETs. Find out their agenda—the truth!

1/12/19 Dream. I was looking for another bowl to do my healings with and a lady named CLARE-ANN-HAVEN told me that the bowl was an N100 and I asked her to make me two more. She said, "In this mining town, we are out of TOPOR which is what we need to make that bowl." I was asked to place my request on a piece of paper. Her name is pronounced CLAREY-ANN. The TOPOR was more expensive than gold.

1/12/19 Continued. Those two guys I saw yesterday, the guy with the double purple glasses and the hairy arms wanted me to see them and they wanted me to feel scared. Why?

1/13/19 I found 20 bruises on each leg and a new one on my right thigh—high up. Bob asked me about the "scars" from being bitten by mosquitoes on 11/24/18-12/2/18—I mistakenly thought they just hadn't healed. BUT, not true! They are bruises from being taken at night. I showed Bob a new one on the right thigh. I told him it was proof that I was being taken against my free will and they used guns. I think the hairy-armed guy's "gun" was what made those bruises on my legs.

1/13/19 Remote view. Mars. Inside there is a mine. I can hear pickaxes tinkling and chinking on the rock. It's orange in there. Shovels.

1/14/19 Last night after I turned out the lights I saw green grass in my eyes. It blotted out everything else. I've never seen that before except in 2009 when I woke up to a green smoke over my bed.

1/16/19 I was in my den and starting having an allergic reaction—itching and eye problems and started using the cancellation tool when someone, "an intermediary," invaded my thoughts to ask me to stand down. I explained that the asshats drove me to these lengths by escalating constantly. He tried to tell me I was escalating too and that they would stop if I would. I told him I didn't believe it because (1) they have been doing things to me my whole life and never once thought to stop and (2) they have proven to me that they are relentless narcissists. Then I kicked him out of my head.

1/16/19 Continued. I think there's a lesson here but I'm not torturing them back. I'm just trying to keep from being tortured constantly and finding out information. They raise the ante with the torture. STOP the TORTURE! This is not a tit for tat situation, which is how they are twisting it. They are eager to show me their superior dominance. They will break any rules to get what they want. Am I bound by any rules?

1/16/19 Continued. I just realized that the ASSHATS want me to give up everything in order for them to STOP. NO! I will never agree to that.

1/16/19 Continued. I am really starting to be able to cancel out a lot of things. Some do not work. Cancellation for diseases didn't work, for instance, but other things did.

1/18/19 Yesterday, I challenged some remote viewers outside to show themselves and they said, "We know what you'll do." I guess the word is out.

1/18/19 Continued. I was told the next time I get scared, to meditate.

1/18/19 Continued. Archangel Michael told me to take the Swerdlow book to my medium and give her an outline so that we could collaborate, help others, and learn from each other. It did not go well.

1/20/19 My medium always talked about the importance of discernment and went on and on about how I could never feel anything but neutrality and that was a defect in myself and I wasn't trying hard enough. She also said that I wiped out the discernment lesson by using these tools. Well, ASSHATS MIMIC, so it is impossible to know a good "click" from a bad "click" (in our ears). I thought the lesson was "there is mimicry" so understand that and use the tool. My need for my medium's mentoring is over. No more mentoring. I am my own mentor.

1/21/19 Remote view for missing time. Brown doorway, long hallway to conference room. Many human military men discussing me. Apparently, when I use the **cancellation tool**, on someone or something, they disappear! I disappeared a doctor, one of their best doctors. They were also discussing me and whether I knew who or what I was—they said no, but they thought they should take me out of the "program." I saw myself face down in an operating room and my back being worked on. I was screaming at them calling them ASSHATS! They also said that I was telling Bob things and he was telling others in his group and causing them to rebel. It might be a good time to take Bob out of the program too.

1/25/19 Remote view. Remote viewed my big bruise on my left leg. There are two or three puncture marks in the middle. I was able to see the asshats in green with guns. They took me to a ship—through a doorway. I was in a clear tube lying down and was carried there sleeping. They put me in this device with clear glass like a capsule. I was put in a big room with other capsules/people and hooked up to a big programming station. We were programmed en masse.

1/25/19 Continued I had someone in the car with me while driving. I could tell because water bottles were cracking as if they were pressure changes. People, entities, ETs, ghosts, etc., dropping in on me, in my car. I think it is discourteous! I told whoever it was that it was RUDE and to GET OUT! They said, "You're angry," and I said, "You would be too if this kept happening to you."

1/26/19 Last night I saw my clock move—I have a projector clock that projects the numbers on the ceiling in red. Last night I was watching the ceiling when the red numbers moved to the right on their own. This is the 2nd time I've seen this. Is this a time slip?

1/28/19 Last night realized that some or all of remote viewers are there for BOB!

1/30/19 Dreams. I had multiple dreams in a row that I was on an animal like an elephant or dinosaur and I was riding it and was in a huge cave of black diamonds or dark shiny stones. Then I felt I could not breathe and I had the same or similar dream and again felt like I couldn't breathe. This happened over and over. I finally woke up to go to the bathroom and saw a huge swirling black smoke thing on my bed. There were white swirls too.

2/1/19 Last night I saw a red line in my room. I spoke to two to three remote viewers asking why they were watching me. One was a Praying Mantis named Jonah. He said he was making sure I was still here and that I leave sometimes to go to other galaxies. Jonah also said I worked in mines.

2/3/19 At 4:21 AM a smoke monster of black and light colored pulsing light sat on me so I could not breathe and then started sucking on me, snuffling my ears and nose. I cancelled him. He was waiting on the side of the room near the window/door. The smoke monster stayed around and I suddenly felt I had to go to the bathroom but I knew it wasn't true—it was a program designed to get me out of bed. So, I was trapped there. I knew someone wanted me out of my house and at another location.

2/3/19 Continued. Spoke to another remote viewer and he said he was human and the layers go like this: ET, human, ET, human. The human at the top is a superhuman.

2/4/19 Snapping noises coming from kitchen. They sound like Mexican jumping beans. I was told they are "invisible beings."

2/4/19 Continued. I was doing a healing on Bob when some "invisible beings" came in and asked what I was doing. They told me they were going to wipe out everyone on Earth with a plague They wanted to know why the remote viewers were watching me and I said I didn't know. They said the remote viewers wouldn't tell them either. They said I might be valuable and they might make me their prisoner. My acupuncturist said that invisible beings were coming from the Sun in droves. Our sun is a stargate

2/4/19 Continued. I found a spot on my face on the right side near the corner of my mouth. Bob has the same spot on the left side of his mouth. I'm going to do a remote view to see where it came from.

2/4/19 Remote view of the spots on our faces. Surgery—in different rooms. They were working on the right side of my brain and Bob's left side. The doctors were human. They were fixing our programming and wondering aloud how I keep breaking mine. They went in through the mouth.

2/5/19 Dream. I had a dream about being held down and screaming. I had a rough night—not sleeping a lot.

2/5/19 Continued. I saw two light dots like eyes in addition to regular blinky lights last night. I also put on my glasses—the lights were closer than I ever thought to my face and bed.

2/5/19 Continued. Found multiple two-pronged bumps on my chest. Maybe a small stun gun? ½ inch apart—similar in structure to the needle marks that put me to sleep. Some are one inch apart and others are ¾ inches apart.

2/5/19 Continued. When I put my glasses on, I found that I could see what I thought was a remote viewer with a round black void, but later, the way it moved, it seemed like a person/being with a round head, a short being. At one point I woke up and I found that my jaw under my right ear really hurt. I think this was an implant. Maybe a new one.

2/7/19 Woke up thinking my teeth had been removed. It felt real so I'm pretty sure it happened.

2/7/19 Continued. I had a dream about being in two bodies at the same time. One was asleep and the other awake.

2/12/19 Contacted MUFON today and filled out their questionnaire.

2/13/19 Woke up with a sty yesterday so I did a remote view to see how I got it:

2/13/19 Remote view: How did I get the eye issue? On a ship. Praying Mantises had my right eye out and they were drilling it. Zzzzt, zzzzt, zzzzzt and there was something stuck on my eyelid. I started waking up and flailing around. They said I was getting strong and they weren't sure what to do. They also said I tried to access the eyeball. The one doctor was a small white/cream colored praying mantis or a grasshopper.

2/18/19 Couldn't sleep until 2 AM Woke up at 3:39 AM—tried to remember and saw a black rectangle—I was taken. Before sleep I felt a light pin prick on my arm. This morning, I felt a scab from a syringe on back of neck.

2/18/19 Remote view of last night's black rectangle: A being came into my room. They used a tool that looked like a woman's disposable razor. It touched my head and I woke up. They touched it in the middle of my forehead. Then, I got up and got dressed. It left through a doorway in the wall, it was rectangular. There was a ship waiting. I went into the ship. The shaver thing closes a loop on the memory. It was silver and shiny and when touched to the head, there are sparks or arcs of electricity.

2/19/19 Someone made my right eye blurry last night at 3 AM and I awoke to find it. Yahweh didn't help but after going back to sleep, someone fixed it.

2/20/19 Spoke with MUFON yesterday. I got leads on UFO contactee groups. There's a new meetup I joined for Sunday, February 24, 2019 for UFOs.

2/20/19 Remote view. I am on a submarine and I'm wearing a white shirt and grey pants. I'm a teacher and I'm teaching people how to remote view. Since I have been doing this my whole life, I'm teaching others the possibilities of the mind. I'm not in the navy but seem to be a civilian, but I'm wearing uniform like clothes. I have a huge engagement ring on my finger and I take it off so my class doesn't tease me. I'm not wearing glasses (thick or otherwise) and they call me Ms. Liz my real Maiden Name. My fiancé is someone I know in real life and he's wearing a white coat. We have separate quarters and there are circular hallways I can trip over. My room has a hammock and a bed. In my class I have meditation music blasting and all of the men are passed out in their desks. I have either a light show or strange visuals to relax their minds. I ask them "Where are you? Are you with me?" I think my age is 25. The, "Say Yes to the Dress" song for that program plays in my head while I see all of this. My ring is HUGE! 2 or 3 carats. A dream I had flashes in my mind, where I was with this guy and my sister, Sarah, in a huge dining room with a buffet and I was wearing my huge ring.

2/21/19 Last night there was a lot of activity. Finally, after being poked multiple times I saw a circle of white—like a flashlight, a small one, the size of a ½ dollar (no beam) near Bob's head and I then felt a sting. My arm started itching and a bump developed, on my left arm on the inside of my elbow. I also heard someone say, "Go to sleep!" I held off as long as I could and finally fell asleep at 2:15 AM-ish. I heard someone say, "She's so stubborn."

2/21/19 Besides the one puncture mark (from sleep syringe) that I have on my arm, the only other mark is a stun gun mark on my chest ¾ inches in length.

2/22/19 Remote view. As a little girl, I was given the code word: Rose Garden. When I heard it, I was to get up and do what I was told and when I heard the words a 2nd time my mind would be erased. The programmer had something hooked up to my head. When it was over I couldn't remember anything. I went to my bunk and talked to my roommate who asked what happened and I couldn't remember. She left to go and see for herself. Later we all (six to nine kids) left our bodies, held hands and flew to another galaxy. It sucked being us.

2/23/19 Went to a UFO meetup today. The guy was Native American and had a following. He spoke of good and bad ETs. I would like to work with the good ones and have good experiences. This guy also spoke about "going to the light" = reincarnation.

2/26/19 Woke up last night twice with what looked like blood in my eyesight. Found out later, that I had holes poked in both eyes. I could only see these marks while waiting for a light to change and concentrating on the back of a car. I could only see these marks when I closed my eyes and had the "negative effect" like seeing a negative. I also found a cut on my belly on the left side about two inches in length.

2/27/19 More phone monkeying around. My phone regularly has dead spots in it, even when I turn it upside down (to work in landscape mode). So annoying. I saw a bright white circle last night, not a flashlight.

2/28/19 Dream. I was programming a variable into a computer and one of the variables was "free" and the other was "recess." I was working with a woman who was new. We gave her a card, everyone signed it. She was leaving. When she left the area, she gave me a hug. The text was:

cmd
Variable "Free"
Variable "Recess"

Am I a programmer?

2/28/19 Continued. At one point last night I saw a black orb. It had white parentheses back to back and inside these parentheses, I saw light green or olive green dots in each.

3/7/19 Woke up at 4 AM. Could only remember black rectangle. I will have to remote view this time period. Woke up with my little finger on my left hand inflamed near the inside of the nail bed. I've found that ET's perform torture or something by shocking the fingers. It is painful but not obvious at first. Unclear what the purpose is. My back hurts today. It is sore and inflamed and stiff. Did they add implants to my back again?

3/7/19 Remote view why my back hurt today: Some large spiral brown hallway. In an operating room. Grasshopper was the surgeon. "She" wanted to know why I keep taking "these" out? "She" said I requested them to be placed there. Others talking. "Maybe she doesn't know she requested it." Suddenly, there was an explosion and smoke coming out of my back. Someone's nose started falling off—it was acidic gas. "We need to ask her again. Why wouldn't she want them? Let's place three of them, two on each side and one in the middle. Someone really hurt her eye. Look what they did to it. I think they're sabotaging us. She couldn't have done this herself. Let's fix her eye."

3/8/19 Dream. A place or company called SKYSKATE. I was saying that it was a game and we were all like avatars moving around a board. There was a car stuffed with people in the back and through the car window, I saw one of the people blink. They were stuffed back there like mannequins. Woke up at 4:44 AM. Didn't feel hot but knew something happened.

3/10/19 Remote view of last night's abduction, who and why. White/green/black three Praying Mantis or Grasshoppers. The white & green had softer features and were smaller. The black one was harder looking, hard shell over body. We are underwater in a jelly like clear pod operating room. There was a hallway connected to it (a brown hallway) where people with uniforms could watch. A carat ^ symbol with two parallel lines underneath was their emblem. The black one said I was an "experiment," going AI, in my eyes, left thigh, left, right, hip and spine. The thing they put in my back for both hips, and spine looked like a dowel about three inches in length with four wings total. Two on the top and two on the bottom. My thigh has a computer chip as does my right eye.

3/10/19 Remote view about what Skyskate is. This is a government project, Project SKYSKATE. Nonsensical name, under water. I saw a long brown hallway, the jelly operating room, and the words: Project SKYSKATE.

3/10/19 Remote view. That song "Don't Bring Me Down" by Electric Light Orchestra was playing. I was in the backyard of Mom & Dad's house, sunbathing. I could feel the sweat running down my back. The sun was out. Then, there's a big tear in the scene—a big black gash. Then, a brown room with brown bunk beds. Everything is brown. That song came out in 1979.

3/11/19 Remote view of black gash in scenery. Back to underground, underwater surgery center. Brain surgery. The same doctor was there: Shaggy. There was also a dark beetle-like praying mantis with a hard shell body.

3/11/19 Remote view. Saw me being held by two reptilians. I'm in a dark, dank, wet underground place. They throw me in a jail cell. I feel RAGE & HATRED for them and I tell them so. I ask WHY? I'm 57 years old! They say I am "special." They say, "If you don't behave we will blast you into unconsciousness." I see someone I know and hate, the person who ruined my computer, so I ran over and grabbed her by the neck and rammed her head into the bars. I hate her! Zap! Darkness.

3/11/19 Remote view. The long brown hallway and brown doors. I'm in a classroom. I'm new. The kids look scared. Next door—screams, then silence. They are testing our skills in the classroom. In the operating room, they have hooked us up to the machines and they have a drill. They drill our scalp and skull and we pass out. They wake us up. A little boy in class told me to go somewhere else in my head. I go there to escape the current pain. The kids all help each other. The doctor tells "Shaggy" not to let my dad go past the operating room. He does and freaks out.

3/13/19 Last night all kinds of tones entered my head. My oversoul told me it was my "preparation tones" that prepares me for abduction. Preprogramming. They weren't working.

3/14/19 Went to meet with that Native American man who has the UFO meetup to discuss having my own meetup group. But he wanted me to come to one of his meetings for a 15 minute talk. It is scheduled for 3/23/19.

3/15/19 Woke up but I was underground. I could see light all around me and darkness. I found myself puzzling over some strangely shaped lights for several minutes before finally realizing I was in my own room.

3/16/19 Wrote outline for talk for UFO meetup on 3/23/19 then wrote a letter to Stewart Swerdlow asking for permission to copy pages out of his book. I thought this talk was on 4/23/19, not 3/23/19)

3/18/19 Took letter to Swerdlow to mailbox and heard someone say, just as I put it in the outgoing mail: "You just sealed your fate."

3/20/19 Woke up at 1:25 AM screaming "GET AWAY FROM ME!" I woke Bob up. I remember a red smoke/fog. I've seen it before on my bed. When I woke up a little, I wasn't scared. My heart wasn't pounding. I told Bob "I saw something!"

3/20/19 Remote view of red cloud and my screaming. I was in a cage in a long hallway. Tons of other people were in cages moaning, crying and screaming. There was a doctor in a white coat with a British accent. He was telling me that this was my true life and the other one was an illusion. My real life was in this cage and they were watching me all the time like a true life *Truman Show*. I am not special, just defiant and if I don't stop they will kill everyone I love. I am helpless and can't change anything. Here I am telling people things and acting like I can affect change. It's impossible. The place smelled dark, dank and must be where I go when I leave. That guy must have been trying to program me. Bastards!

3/20/19 Dream. Was talking to a friend and her name was INAME3.

3/20/19 – had to go to CA – my father is in Hospice.

3/26/19 My poor father has all kinds of marks on his arms—like blood blisters. He says they "appear but don't hurt." Sounds suspicious to me.

3/26/19 Remote view. Wanted to see who or what was taking me while at my father's bedside. All black figure with yellow eyes. Unsure what that is.

4/9/19 Had a dream about being at a party and eating a bright blue cookie. I was told it was good but I didn't think it was all that great. Then, I ate something that looked like quiche. Woke up with food in my teeth on left side only.

4/20/19 Last night I saw a new eye thing. This one has black/white stripes and it affects both eyes and is bright whether eye is closed or open. I can still turn it off by turning my head to the right.

4/20/19 Continued. Last night there was a terrifying presence and they were stopping me from speaking to my oversoul. It was so oppressive and terrifying. I had to ask for help from Archangel Michael and was told I would be helped as long as I needed it. As soon as I started asking for help the terrifying feelings stopped and I felt normal. These presences were not physical and they are worse than humans or the ETs in charge of our planet now. Their presence/feeling took over my house and I realized that they were the reason my house felt off when I returned to my house on 4/16/19. I had to clear the house and felt betrayal, insecurity, and anxiety. It was the entities in the house affecting me until I cleared it using my bowl. Whatever and whoever these large/massive/heavy/menacing presences were last night, they really scared me. They were more frightening than anything I've encountered up till now.

4/20/19 Remote view of what comes out of TV when turned on. Black figures, lots of them. As soon as the TV turns on, they flood the room.

4/21/19 Remote view of terrifying presences. Dark cloaked figures surrounding me. They walked into my dimension as if it were a transparent green wall. They were called "The Disciples." They knew I was getting stronger and they were here to stop me. When I asked for help, a big green shield surrounded me and they dissipated.

4/22/19 Dream. I was in a house with other women. There was a phone under me. I had a baby on my lap. The phone rang. It was my mother. A big white spotlight appeared next to me. The girl next to me was trying to get out of the spotlight. The phone rang under me. I picked it up and my mother was asking me if I liked the baby. I said I knew if I tell her I like it, she'll use it against me. There was a helicopter noise. I hung up the phone but they could still hear us talking.

4/22/19 Remote view. In a warehouse—2nd story—surrounded by men in black fatigues, all black with helmets and dogs and guns. The spotlight is an alien ship.

4/25/19 Woke up at 2:19 AM. Didn't know WHO I was or WHERE I was. Then I remembered: I was Lisa of Lisa & Bob.

4/25/19 Continued. Found some loose skin on left pinky finger outside cuticle and pulled it off—it revealed painful red area—very painful—too painful for the small amount of skin removed.

4/27/19 Dream. Had a dream about Dad. I was carrying him and he had on a shirt, that was sewn shut. I carried him to a shallow cave and cut his shirt off, cutting through the stitches. The shirt was plaid and the stitches were green.

4/27/19 Remote view of dream. My dream about my dad in the cave means that Dad was a slave. You can't get your clothes off because they are sewn onto you depicting your slave status. By cutting off Dad's shirt, I freed him. He was no longer a slave.

5/1/19 – Arturians. Met with an Arturian hybrid for guidance. The Arturians have zero tolerance for abductions so I am safe. NOT. They wanted information, which I would provide and then, they would let anyone and everyone take me. I learned an important lesson working with them. Whenever you work with another entity, you must ask for something in exchange or ask what they want in exchange. The rest of the universe does not use money, so it's barter. I thought I was asking for protection in exchange for information, but ... I was giving money to their hybrid for guidance which isn't the same thing.

5/4/19 Dream. Had dreams in light language. It was gold with bright white around it.

5/6/19 Dream. Had a dream where I was trying to scream but couldn't.

5/7/19 Woke up twice to my room with all the lights on. I was waiting for instructions each time. Unclear what instructions.

5/10/10 Found an experiencer support group. I hope this is a gateway for my healing tools.

5/12/19 At 3:10 AM I flew back into my body and started a coughing fit that lasted 20 minutes. I think my landing was harsh, not smooth.

5/14/19 Dream. I was getting liposuction and they were starting with my right arm. They stuck me with something that looked like a stick pin (the kind with the ball on the end but with ½ of the ball). It was sharp and it hurt. Then there was a line (tube for blood) coming out of it. After a while my arm got very skinny. I pulled it out and there was a whole apparatus. I pulled it all out and left it on the floor. I was in room A102 in a hotel called A10. I shared the room with several people. There was a woman in the bed near my head who needed comforting. She was crying. Later another guy was in the bed near me and he was very tall. He wanted to show me the city. He took me out of the hotel room and when I was out, I remembered going in and it seemed a lot different. Initially, the hallway was red and white striped, like a candy cane. But now it was very dark, like a dark copper maze. We saw a moving pharmacy that had many doors and they would open and help people on the street. There were many people.

5/19/19 Remote view of bruises I found on my collarbone. Asshats programmed my head. I received two shots, one near my right eye. One in my collarbone with a huge syringe. Men in black army outfits with insignias, that looked like a Leo astrology symbol with one line underneath it got me. They said, "This one's a fighter." Then, in real life, I heard high pitched noises in my ear and pressure change—so I cancelled them out.

5/19/19 Woke up at 4:04 AM with my left inside forearm hurting and the left side of my neck itching. The arm hurt so much that I turned on LaHoChi and I did a healing plus touched that arm. This morning there are two red marks on it. They are slight and hard to see. There is a scratch plus a dot.

5/21/19 Woke up twice. Felt extreme negativity and hopelessness. I cancelled out what I could. They wanted me to feel that I'm not getting anywhere and I never would. This makes me feel good. I must be getting somewhere. I didn't wake enough to know this at the time.

5/21/19 Remote view of extreme negative entities. 1st group—could not see them—only hear them. Programmers plus one guy talking about who and what I am—an asset. I have blocked off part of my own brain where they used to program me. "Boss": "Find out who and what are doing this!" 2nd group—guy with glasses and beard. "Who is messing with MY Discovery? Someone else has made changes—someone has been here before US! Find out who they are." Could only hear the rest. Dr. Asshat is complaining to military guy that they are the only one's allowed to touch me. Complaining to find out who. These two groups felt horrible and violent and negative.

5/21/19 Continued. Saw giant Praying Mantis shadow doing something wildly in the air. I cancelled it out. Next time I'll get up and look at it.

5/22/19 Saw something in the corner of my room, near my bed last night—tried to cancel it out, could not, so I got up and looked at it.

I immediately saw red plus bright green and everything looked fuzzy. The room where I was got very bright then darkened. I slept like a log. My dreams were fragmented. Something about being in a group and climbing around a being in line for food. A person asked me to throw one so I did and it landed on his head (a pizza). When standing up looking at things in my room last night, I also saw invisible beings moving around. I tried to touch one but could not feel anything. I could see it in contrast to the room.

5/22/19 Remote view. I saw the place with the brown buildings, yellow lights in the buildings, a big cave. It's a program but not a hologram. It seems real and feels real. It's on the moon. That's where this place is located. Inside the buildings programs run. We are watched by remote viewers to see how we'll react.

5/23/19 Woke up multiple times. Was left with an inch scratch on my right top forearm and my left belly area.

5/23/19 Remote view of who, what and where I got those injuries: Walked down a dark and dank hallway where two wolves appeared and ended up right into a cage. A metal one. There was another woman either in the cage or next to my cage. She said, "Have you been a bad girl?" I said "Yep! I'll never learn." And then we gave each other fist bumps that ended with fingers waving and intertwining with each other. She wanted to know what I would do next but I told her "the walls have eyes and ears but it will be EPIC." She asked: "Was it worth it?" I said, "Yes."

5/23/19 I saw a purple/lavender flower instead of an eyeball in my room last night.

5/25/19 Met with a MUFON experiencer investigator. She told me to write this book.

5/25/19 Found a new bump. The skin is raised and there is a bit of skin off the top. It doesn't hurt.

5/25/19 Remote view of how I got the bump. I was brought there by big spiders. They are pets of Reptilians. Saw a black guy in white military outfit (ball cap, not helmet). That's all.

5/26/19 Kept waking up with my night guard in my hand.

5/26/19 Remote view of night guard incident(s). I could see one black guy with a mustache in white military garb. I was on a cot and they were pumping me full of liquid with a big ribbed hose. The hose was opaque. It was hard to see anything. They do not want me to see this. I will continue to work on this.

5/26/19 Remote view of black guy in military garb. Insignia is a vertical WV with the points pointing left with three dots in the wide areas. They were silver stitching on white. These "people" were spiders. They were different—white with no hair on legs. The "black" guy was sucking fluid out of me, not putting it in. They had me in a tank of fluid and there was an apparatus for me to breathe. Something covered my mouth and nose—like for SCUBA diving. There were bubbles around my head. Telepathically, they were questioning me... "How did you get rid of the other spider group?" "What did you do to them?" This group is negative as well and they have three eyes and that's who is looking at me in my room when I mistakenly thought it was the "good guys." When they were sucking fluid out of me, I was on what looked like a cot and the "black guy" was moving his lips to pretend to talk to me when he was really using his mind.

5/27/19 Dream. I was in the building on the first floor. It was very bright and there was a variegated violet dot there. I was on a mission. There was a guy trying to block my exit. Everything on this floor of the building was white, even the clothing of the guy blocking me. I went out another exit to avoid being caught. The guy was disappointed that I would get away. As I walked outside and tried to cross the street, there were many cars all spaced out and I looked up to see military guys in white wearing a captains' hats crossing the street in the crosswalk to get to the building I had just vacated. They saw me. I was trying to figure out how to get back in the building the next day and was thinking of shaving my head. During this dream I smell something like peanut butter but I called it "dark peanut butter" or "dark smelling peanut butter."

5/28/19 Had a big yellowish/green light in upper left corner of room—pulsing. I then felt a stealthy poke in my right forearm. I looked up and saw a child-sized human head jump off the right corner of the bed. I got really scared and started calling out for my guides to help. At the time this happened I was thinking about my book and how I would organize it and whether or not I would try my hand at self-publishing. I suddenly saw a black thing fly by my head and I saw several disks blinking. I woke up at 3:24 AM and felt myself lightly touching down on the bed.

5/30/19 Thinking about the book/organization of it, how I want to put it all together, etc., bring out the asshats in full force.

5/30/19 I saw many things—one was a type of flashing light that wasn't very bright. It was two people flashing—click, click to each other. The light did not go far—it wasn't a flashlight, just a white circle—just stayed across from each other. I have seen flashlights with pieces of paper over them to diffuse the light. I'll see it go on and go off, like a signal. They are round and white but not a torch.

5/30/19 Continued. I also saw a red arc with two red humps.

5/30/19 Continued. I could not sleep until 6 AM. As I did finally fall asleep, I saw two eyes, staring at me from the top of the curtain rod near the ceiling. It was like a portal, shaped like a vertical barbell or goggles, so that when you're lying down, you can see it. These portal goggles go the entire length of the curtain rod and I could see the first one best when I closed one eye. All sort of voyeurs were there watching me. I saw human eyes and other-worldly eyes but only the two eye variety. All sorts of two-eyed being were watching me. I tried cancelling it out, and it would dim a bit but I could still see it.

6/3/19 Started Extended Remote Viewing online course. Discovered that the membrane is the popping noise when you are at your target.

6/3/19 Remote view. Went to doorway. Many rooms with big wide tall plastic as walls/doors. Two individuals working on me. I could not see them at first. Eventually, I could. One was a white spider—hairless, standing upright. I did not see the face. The 2nd being was a beetle. Their people suits are: black guy with insignia = white hairless spider and Dr. Peterson (Shaggy) with long hair and glasses = beetle! They intercepted me on my way to something else. They knew my programming was changed and/or missing and new programming was being blocked. They know that big hairy spiders are stealing me and removing/replacing things and changing what is in my eye. I wonder if Shaggy has been a beetle all along?

6/6/19 Felt something on my arm last night. Woke up at 4:14 AM, only I didn't know I was awake or asleep. I was somewhere else. But I was changing the cancellation affirmation while looking at a grid of some sort. On the grid there was white on pink. It was either milk or a sheet of something thin. While seeing this, I was changing. The only reason I woke up from my in between state is because my cat meowed loudly on the right side of the bed.

6/6/19 Remote view being taken from sleep to 4:14 AM. I was taken to a ship. It was very clean and very quiet. No people/beings. In another room, I see two beings that look like white light in people form. They are at "controls" near a bank of windows. Then, I see myself in another room. I am wearing some of my clothes and they are looking me over and scanning me. They find the "thing" in my right outside forearm and pull it out.

6/9/19 Taken mid-thought! Found some bruises on my buttocks. These were torture sessions and were a message about not using Extended Remote Viewing. I also found needle marks that resembled numbers or brands. They were three and nine on my left leg.

6/11/19 My acupuncturist said to use the golden triangle because it's very powerful. Yes! Needed that!

6/12/19 Dream. I was doing a remote view for Microsoft. It was a Wednesday and I wrote that on my paper. I was blocked and could not remote view, even though I had a huge paragraph of things I saw, words of description.

6/17/19 Spirit guides say I have all the tools I need to stop abductions. Just need to use them.

6/19/19 Got menaced. The fear was intense—before sleep. There were Praying Mantises in the corner and I saw various red things near the bookcases. I called for help. I told Bob what was going on because he couldn't see it or feel it. This pissed them off and it got VERY scary in there. The fear was intense. I kept cancelling out those in my room. It cleared out. I fell asleep and woke up at 2 AM. It was cleared out but there was a rainbow colored swatch with dots and a dark shadow pushed it into a hole and everything was quiet.

6/19/19 Continued. Found a stun gun mark on the tip of my nose. They seemed pissed when I was teaching LaHoChi to people. Too bad! They all showed up when I asked Bob to practice his LaHoChi on me.

6/21/19 I was told by my spirit guides to give my sister, Sarah, a LaHoChi attunement when I stayed with her. I did it. That night, sleeping in her bed with her, I woke up to Sarah touching my hand, twice, and saying to me "You don't have to go." I would not have remembered if she hadn't touched me.

6/27/19 Did not feel anything last night but I have a new bruise on my left knee. It's a slightly round bunch of dots with one in the middle. They are syringe marks.

6/27/19 Continued. I was REMOVED from my car while I was driving! I was merging onto the freeway. I drive a stick. It was unnerving and annoying!

6/27/19 Remote view for my chronic neck pain. Me spread-eagle on a metal bed. A big metal arm with needles on the end. One needle on each end. One near my lady parts and one in the left side of my neck. There is purple liquid in the needles. The entity administering it was a large black spider with a white face masks and a black hood. The body type was black widow. The pain I have in my neck is venom and I was stuck in both places on my left side.

6/29/19 Woke up at 2 AM looking at the clock projected on the ceiling and I saw two faces looking at me. They were red like the clock. I wasn't sure if I was really seeing them until each one blinked. They were human. I was told by my spirit guides that they want me to feel like they are more powerful than me. Ok. I'm afraid, but I'm NEVER giving up!

7/1/19 Dream. I had a dream that I woke up at 3:56 AM—it was about my mortality and how I had a sheath over my entire body. I felt the feeling of knowing my age and seeing the years get closer and dying. It was a weird feeling. I could see that I was a light body underneath.

7/4/19 Woke up with a smoke monster in the room and I said, "I'm not going. I have free will. I do not choose to leave my bed."

7/8/19 Dream. I was in a huge hospital looking for Dr. Nakamura—an eye doctor. There was a blonde woman in handcuffs in a white car. She was handcuffed to the ceiling of this car or golf cart. The "hospital" was huge and had large blue/wide carpeting that pointed, like a path to various areas. The floor was bright white and the ceiling was about 20 ft. The place looked like a warehouse with white floor and people with white coats on, milling around.

7/8/19 Remote view of dream. I was in the hospital I dreamed about. I was also handcuffed to the ceiling. They took me to a room. A white military man who looked like the Terminator of the movie *Terminator 2* but had short sandy brown hair, and was wearing a green/olive uniform. His eyes were blue/white. He hit me over and over on the area where my tooth was pulled for a tooth implant and my right jaw became swollen on that area. He wanted to know what they told me. "What did they tell you What did they show you? You know more." I called him an asshole and mentioned the memory erasing. He hit me again. When I saw Shaggy, the doctor with the white coat, long hair, beard and glasses, using a syringe, he shot me with something. I also saw brown insects. They were helping them. They looked like Praying Mantises with long brown bodies—two segment abdomen and an upside-down triangle for a head.

7/8/19 Remote view. Jupiter in the red dot. Straight down a hole to a mining area with tracks for mining cars. Could hear voices—could not understand language. It was murmuring. Mining gold. The cave was reddish-orange—like iron or rust.

7/8/19 Continued. I have never been able to cancel Shaggy. Yet.

7/9/19 Remote view. I'm in a bed. Another programmer works on me. A spider in a human suit. I have been reprogramming myself. I have one alter. They use long needles near my eyes and elsewhere use a clear tablet to program my brain. I took out the program, the one in my eye. They will have to redo it. They fired the other programmer because I could undo it. I am a smart and talented programmer. No wonder they chose me for abductions. The person talking to the programmer was a human in a green uniform. The insignia looked like a vertical DNA symbol but with no ladder.

7/10/19 Each time I try to cancel out a sleeping device the song by Queen "Don't Stop Me Now" comes on. I started singing "Neutron Dance" by The Pointer Sisters, whenever "Don't Stop Me Now" comes on. Each time I try to cancel out anything in my mind, that same song comes on. So, I sing my own song. Play bitch games, get bitch prizes.

7/11/19 – Remote view of the incident where my sister touched me twice and said, "You don't have to go," when I was staying with her and I wanted to find out why. Black peanut-shaped head with red eyes that glow. They used a switch (like a light switch) to get me to leave with them.

7/12/19 Took a picture of a large bruise I got on my right calf. It looked like a brand or initials of SP. This bruise isn't new. The initials showed up today. JP or SP—unclear what this means.

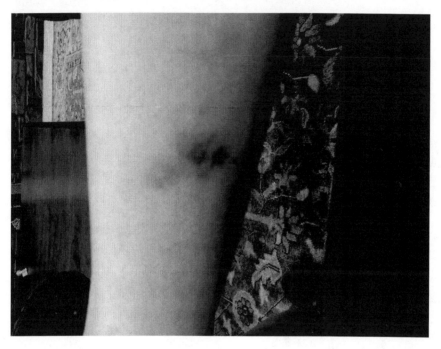

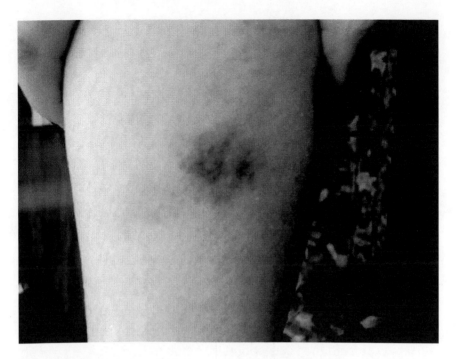

7/16/19 Dream. I walk into a room in a big building. I'm on the ground floor. The room is made of glass. I walk in and other women are there. The room has a bed. I am trapped in there. The other women try to comfort me. The glass has a one way mirror. People can't see in, we can see out. They house women and children in this room. One woman offers sex to make me feel better. I get out of this room/building and I can see in but the women can't see out. I see a woman I want to save. She can't see me. I pound on the window and try to see her in the crack of two windows that came together. Then I hear that a woman with brown hair in a bun/ponytail is chasing me. I run off. I find a big white ball with handles and I use it to get away from them. It works and the ball lets me float fast and high. Bob, my husband, is with me and we start to touchdown because the ball needs a charge. Bob and I are running and we meet someone to ask about the ball and the guy says, "Did you get this at a party?" I felt a knife in my hand and shoved it into someone and continued running. Then, I lost Bob. Later I went back to the guy to find Bob and the person I stabbed. Another guy said he had some of "our" hydrogen peroxide and did I want to use it? I took the knife out of the wound and poured the peroxide in the wound. It fizzed. Bob stepped out of the shadows with the woman who was chasing us. He was with THEM, not ME. This husband was very thin. He was wearing a green shirt and khaki pants. It might have been someone who looked like my husband or who they wanted me to think was him so that I would come back for him.

7/16/19 Aftermath of writing this dream down. I had a coughing fit while writing down this dream, so I know they don't want me to remember this and they don't want me to write it down. I think they control our bodies. It's not just programming. It's something else. Maybe hypnosis? I also started itching because I cancelled out the coughing.

7/19/19 Dream. There are three types of memory. (1) Absolute: where no memories get out, (2) Gravitas: where memories get out, and (3) Regular: all memories get out. I was shown a hand to indicate that from the ½ way point in the palm to the fingers = solid black memories, the rest of the palm to the wrist = memories that get out, wrist on down the arm = regular memories.

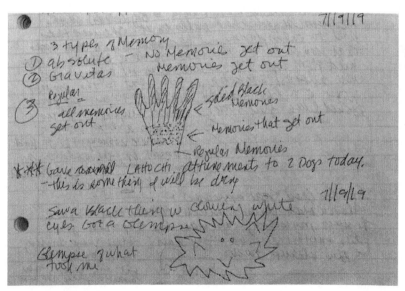

7/19/19 Before sleep. Caught a glimpse of something that abducted me. Black thing with glowing white eyes. It looked like a black sheet where you could see arms moving around under the sheet. But no arms appeared.

7/19/19 After sleep. When I woke up, I remembered aspects of leaving my bed. I kept seeing a scene all night of me, sitting up in bed with a small amount of light around me. This represented to me the amount of times I had been taken which equaled four. My oversoul said it was 20 and helped me get a glimpse of what was taking me and I remembered there was a weird tone and I felt a "crack."

7/21/19 Read *Communion* by Whitley Strieber. What a goldmine of information!

7/22/19 Eyeball holes. Someone poked holes in my right eye last night. They were big and looked like a snowflake pattern. When I went into the bathroom, I saw the holes and red iris as a reflection or a negative. There was a yellowish-green glow around the iris.

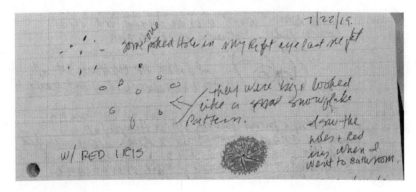

7/22/19 When planes/vehicles go over my house—tones in my ears start up.

7/23/19 Dream. I was in a hospital bed with another guy. The two beds were pushed together and we had IVs. We both had "terminal diseases."

7/24/19 Woke up saying this: Two wicks per day. Diamonds.

7/25/19 Woke up saying this: AI is the cover up.

7/25/19 Remote view for issue with my night guard. I kept taking it out and waking up and finding it in my hands. Could not see anything but could hear things. Peterman or Peterson was supposed to be getting me to drink something but I would not. Then they suggested to me that my teeth had fallen out or there was something wrong with my teeth. Then they gave me something to eat instead. I only chewed on my left side. There were some problems with my programming and they couldn't fix it. Someone yelled, "FIX it, Master Sergeant."

7/25/19 2nd Remote view. Saw water. I was struggling in the water. Heard voices. "What happened?" "She lost all of her training, sir. She doesn't remember anything. This is happening in other areas too. Everything is new to her." I was in a tank. I was told to breathe water. I could not do it. The water is clear like a pool. There are bubbles. "She doesn't know who we are. It's like she's changed." The tank was like an aquarium with clear walls.

7/27/19 After sleep. Found weird bruise on back of right calf. It looks like a paw print shape with syringe/needle marks. It could also be a handprint, but has 5 total bruises/marks.

7/28/19 Dream. I was in a room with women doctors. They were talking to each other about doing medical procedures. One woman challenged the one doctor as to where she was doing the procedures and the other doctor said "nope" and I couldn't see what they were looking at but they were tracing their fingers on a CD case. It was black and smoky brown. They were talking about the hippocampus. It started out like a gynecological procedure but ended up in the hippocampus.

7/28/19 Continued. I cancelled out all programming/procedures with the hippocampus. I got a "yes" from my oversoul.

7/28/19 Dream. Had a dream about Mr. Lydell. He was doing brainwashing techniques. I cancelled him and others like him. Got a "yes."

7/30/19 Remote view. I had an argument with Bob and he got so agitated that I thought it was unusual and decided to remote view the situation. Saw a big black spider with wings zapping Bob and making him agitated. Bob got so upset that I challenged him and was right that he left the room. The spider was large, dark black, standing on two legs but had eight. It had dark wings.

7/31/19 Dream. Had a dream about pus coming out of my face underneath my right eye. It was not like a zit but a huge arc of pus.

7/31/19 Remote view of the pus dream. I find the room where I am on a concrete slab, like a bench. A silver glowing being and humans are surrounding me. They are placing something flat and wide on my face and under my eye. They are attaching it to the back of my head, left side. They are doing this because I continue to turn off the recording where my right eye turns on. They add the pointy things back in my left eye. There was a Reptilian shape-shifter (turns into a human) watching behind a glass. He's the "human" I see in most remote views. He has deep set eyes, crew cut, sandy hair. He is usually in military garb. He might be in charge of me. This same guy was in another room when I was being reprogrammed and my brain was fixing itself.

8/1/19 Dream. I had a dream that my mother led me into my garage where there was a van. The van had people and upright vacuums. My spirit guides led me to this particular dream/screen memory. Using a remote viewing technique, I saw the following:

8/1/19 Remote view. A ship, above my house, near the garage with a light that sucked me into a ship. I could not see anyone's faces, but I did see inside the ship and it was very clean, white with large windows. I was taken to the bowels of the ship, where there were cages and cages of people. The cages were reddish brown and there were women, children, men, babies in these cages. Mothers were trying to comfort their children. They were all crying, in despair, moaning. There were maybe 10 levels of these cages and hundreds or thousands of people. I was placed in a cage as well.

We are all going to the "Programming Center" to be programmed. Reptilians are doing this to us.

8/2/19 Before sleep. Saw a large Praying Mantis in my room. It was in the corner waving it's arms all around. I could see the shadow and the movement.

8/2/19 Remote view of blank spot. Went to Mars, on the other side there is a structure. My memory was removed. The entity who removed my memory was Reptilian. This is all I could see—for now.

8/3/19 While awake. Just a saw a black, white, and yellow creature in Bob's closet. It looked kind of like a cross between a big black spider and an aboriginal being with face paint. It was standing on two legs.

8/4/19 After abduction. Woke up at 5:01 AM today. The only thing I remember just prior to waking up was floating items. I also found a syringe mark on the inside of my mouth on the roof (soft area) on the left. It took a while to fall back asleep and had to do LaHoChi to do so. The area with the syringe mark hurt.

8/4/19 Dream. I had a dream of someone in a white coat painting my teeth with a substance. It looked light lavender and this doctor painted each tooth. I woke up with my right lower jaw/molar inflamed and puffy.

8/4/19 During meditation Sensed a big black, white, and yellow spider. I didn't see it, I felt it. Cancelled it.

8/4/19 After meditation. Saw my right eye thing pop and then it disappeared.

8/5/19 Dream. Could not scream—my mouth would not open. Cancelled out those situations.

8/6/19 Dream. Had a dream that I asked for a LaHoChi attunement and got one in my eye and my eye turned purple. The place was dark and the whites of my eyes were bright and then I got the lavender/florescent "attunement." Woke up at 2:28 AM.

8/6/19 While reading *Incident at Devil's Den* by Terry Lovelace. Saw a tall completely black shadow with outline walking towards me. I also saw a woman in a brown/beige apron that went over her entire outfit with two ties, one around the neck and one around the waist. She was walking towards me. Saw a 3rd person, a man, near Bob on the couch. I only saw his head and torso, walking around.

8/8/19 Before sleep. Was menaced. Fell asleep really late—like 5 AM. I had started writing this book on 8/7/19.

8/9/19 Before sleep. Menaced again. Cancelled them out and they kept coming back.

8/10/19 Remote view for blanks last night. Military shape-shifters took me. Green uniform. A high-level one—the same one and it's a Reptilian. The insignia is a vertical DNA symbol with dots in the circular areas. Shaggy was there. Shaggy is a human. They think I've had my memory erased too many times.

8/15/19 Before sleep clues. Went to bed at 11:34 PM. At 12:09 AM I started hearing the noises from the remote viewers. I heard loud cracks, some sounded like they were coming from the roof and were loud and forceful like an earthquake. I cancelled out what I could. I could see the familiar yellowish-green pulsing light that comes in near the windows with our heavy blackout curtains, indicating their presence. I could feel them in my bedroom waiting for me to fall asleep. As I was laying there I felt the familiar sleep sting on my shoulder. After a few minutes, I got up, put on my slippers, because scorpions, and walked to the bathroom. While sitting there, I briefly looked up and saw a light gray, tall, slender being. It didn't look all that tall—maybe 5'7" and it was standing near the area of the clothes hamper, about 10 feet away. When it realized I was awake it disappeared into thin air.

8/15/19 Continued. This makes me wonder—do I just fall asleep and then get up, put my slippers on, put on clothes and then I leave? After the sleep sting I did not hear anything unusual, feel anything unusual, think anything unusual, but I was not afraid. What did I do that made them think I was asleep and ready to go? Was it that I was not fearful? It also makes me wonder if I had just gotten up and put on clothes, what would have happened? What would I have seen? Next time!

8/15/19 Continued. I woke up at 2:08 AM I was hot.

8/15/19 Morning clues. This morning as I lay in bed thinking about my book, things I should put in and organization, I, as usual, hear the remote viewers. I cancel them out but while lying there, I suddenly move my head on the pillow. I HIT something. It was hard, not my headboard and it had a corner. Was a remote viewer on my bed holding something to my head? Were they trying to hear my thoughts? Or what? Then, another crack—ET remote viewer. I cancel it out. Then I get a zap of electricity on my right foot in the arch. Cancel that out too. The zap on my foot stops. I woke up with plaque on my teeth. I brush my teeth before bed. My first thought was that I missed a spot, but that's not it. It keeps happening. I have a night guard because I grind my teeth, but I still have plaque. Why?

8/15/19 During the day. While driving, I find poke marks in my right eye. It looks like a triangle with extra poke marks on the points of the triangle. Hundreds of poke marks. I can only see it when I'm hit in the eye with the glare of another car where the sun hits it.

8/15/19 Remote view of poke marks. Taken somewhere by Reptilian shape-shifter who looks like a human. I was spread-eagle on a table surrounded by other people. My eyes were poked by thin needs until they were bloody. Was told I was an example.

8/16/19 Remote view to see what made me eat something. Here I thought I'd see people, but no. All I could see were black spider-like things. They were hissing. They came to mind immediately and told me to go back. They were like hissing watch dogs. I had a feeling of great foreboding. I thought about it a bit and did go back. These scenes popped into my head immediately. Usually, I do the exercise completely and then wait for something to pop into my head. This was immediate. I didn't even finish the exercise before I got a picture. Usually, I do the exercise and pay the consequences for my actions later, and I usually feel neutral—as if no punishment is forthcoming. This time was different. I felt immediately that I should not go there. My oversoul said they were a very old race of ETs, but would not divulge anything else. Why would they make me eat something?

8/18/19 After sleep. Woke up with two bruises on the back of my head. They were three inches apart.

8/18/19 Remote view of bruising on back of head. Back to the hissing spiders. Saw a silver metallic arm hanging from the ceiling that has two needles on it. The arm is long and shiny. The back of my head is attached to the needles and I have divots in my head where my head was hooked to this arm with needles.

Book writing! I haven't had time to do anything but this book.

9/6/19 Dream. I was in a law firm. I worked there and suddenly was TERMINATED. The dream was strange in that I was living in this law firm and had a room upstairs. I was told that I was terminated. There was a black and white typed letter with blank underlines left for someone to write in the reason for the termination. The "reason" was written in blue ink, in cursive. I was terminated for "not following instructions." Hmmm. We can only hope. I will remote view this dream later and let you know who and what this is about for my next book. Stay tuned.

As you can see—writing things in notebooks can be helpful. Especially for YOUR book.

There are very scary entities that I have yet to write about. Although, I have had many experiences with this group, I had to leave all of that out because I have not yet **cancelled** them out of my life. They were next on my list when I decided to write this book. I cannot write about them and allow them to punish me with horrific physical illnesses or injuries. It's bad enough that they are mad about this book, but for it to be about them also....I will include all of that in my next book as well as what I'm doing and how I'm getting there.

Onward!

CHAPTER 33
LEARN FROM ME

Be a detective. I don't have all the answers. A lot of times I just have questions. But, I'm figuring it out all the time. Don't let that stop you from seeking answers.

I used to hear tones in my ears or clicking all the time. They still pop up now and then but are mostly gone. I have determined that all or most of the tones are negative. The same for any Morse code you hear in the shower, from lights or machinery or anywhere else. These codes are not in our favor.

Read everything you can because you never know where there's a clue you need buried in a book that applies to your situation.

Never assume anything or anyone is positive. **Cancel** and if it remains, either it's good or you don't have enough information about it. Keep your guard up always. I use the saying: When in doubt, don't do.

Use these tools in the shower. For some reason all entities, remote viewers, ghosts, etc., seem to visit me in the shower. I don't know if it's the water or what. I've felt tingles in the shower, had negative experiences, entities, yahoos talking to me, etc. But, since I can't trust anything or anyone, I use the cancellation tool—every time. We don't know what they are doing to us. Cancel when in doubt.

You're probably wondering why I didn't give you the exact formula I use for cancelling the asshats. Well, the truth is, I did. In a draft early on in the writing of this book, I typed in my exact words. I typed in my formula for cancelling out the asshats, even though I knew that giving them any information would be to my detriment and the next day, no cancellation worked. They blocked me in some way. I was very upset and I know they did this so that they could stop me and they could make me give up and feel defeated. It was painful. It was growth, but painful growth.

I had a setback and had to regroup. But, I am back on track. Many people, me included, want to give you more information, but we can't because then they'll know and block it.

Now, I did have that setback, and I learned SO much! **This is the mindset you need to keep going. You will make mistakes. Learn from them.** Write it all down so that you can remember everything.

This is the dilemma we all face. Who should we tell and how much information? I can feel the pain of other authors right now.

CHAPTER 34
DON'T GIVE UP AND LET'S HELP EACH OTHER

This is not the 50-yard dash as someone recently said to me. This is your life. Work on this when you can, but regularly. Put some effort in. You will be glad you did. You will have many disjointed clues but keep at it because the more you cancel and remote view, the better the picture gets. And you feel better because now they are the guinea pigs. You might still be one, but they are too. Doesn't it feel great?!

But, here's something that needs to be said. We could really help each other if we shared information. This is the reason I am even writing this book—to get this information—my experiences—to the most people possible. We need to share information more, be more open.

Join a support group. Join MUFON. Join the Opusnetwork.org. Opus Network has an email digest where others like yourselves post about their experiences. Admit to others that this happened to you. Write your own book. Make the abduction topic mainstream. Share what you know with others. Share your clues, your weird stories. I bet there's someone out there like me who has had the same experiences but could not put the clues together. We need each other.

Reiki, an energy healing modality is mainstream. Why? Because, people talked about it to others and word spread. Most people now have heard of Reiki. This is the same. Together we can solve this. But it's impossible if we're scattered around scared and silent. Everyone is scared. Me included.

After my setback I did a remote view, using a different tool that I won't mention here for obvious reasons. Here's what I saw

8/11/19 Remote view: A military guy beat me up for months, tortured me and cut me up for defying him. He said "**I own you.**

You don't own you. I'm in charge. You're not." I was stabbed multiple times and they sent me back here. They made me go through all that and then wiped my memory.

CHAPTER 35
A FEW THOUGHTS

If you made it this far, congratulations! It's been a crazy ride. Am I finished, am I ET/abductor free? No. Not yet. I'm still working on it.

I stopped the book here because I was cut off by my spirit guides. No more seeing—this book needed to get out.

I wrote this book so that I could help people like me. I could have used it myself and never told anyone, but I wanted to help us all out.

It's my path to write this book. I was guided. Abductees need hope. We need a way out. It can feel isolated, lonely and as if we are helpless and unable to help ourselves. It's not true. You have to do the work, but it's worth it.

I hope you have categorized your abductors and have been systematically cancelling them all out. I'm down to the last ¼ of my "asshats" and hope to be finished with them soon. I'm also getting a better picture of the truth. I continue to learn things and go forward. This is key.

I have found that we are given as much of the "truth" as we can handle at any given time. And I think this is the reason that some of the remote views show us one thing then shifts later. Our perceptions shift. Our dreams/memories shift. More of the truth peeks out. Now, we can ask better questions. This is all important for your path and your journey. Don't give up and don't judge yourself—you will see some crazy stuff. I had to type from my own journals some remote views/dreams that I seriously considered leaving out because they sound nuts. So, think of me when you're afraid to write this stuff down.

If you are scared every night, me too. But, the only way out is through. I never understood this reference until this experience. You have to go through it to become whole.

If your experiences differs from mine, that's ok. We are all different. When I first contacted MUFON and the experiencer investigator told me that she had never heard what I told her before, I thought at first, OH NO! But, then, I thought—this is my experience, not anyone else's. Use my experiences to help you figure things out. Maybe something I've written about here will help you.

I wanted to clear up that if you have someone in your life that either doesn't believe you or isn't having the experiences you have, don't feel bad. I have found with my husband that I sometimes need a break from this excitement. I need to be grounded. I need to feel normal, like my old self, before I knew about all of this. I sometimes need to forget about it and not be in my head all the time. There is also—life—that gets in the way. I appreciate his role. His experience is different. It actually keeps me sane.

It is also possible that your significant other is programmed to discount your feelings/thoughts and to give out scientific explanations to you. We are all programmed in some way and it can be frustrating and annoying to try to get that person to see what you're seeing. I'm with you. It is frustrating. But, try to keep it in perspective. I've stopped showing Bob my bruises and trying to make him see it. He's not going to. I have to accept that.

The other thing I wanted to say is that wherever you are in this process is the correct time.

Society puts time pressures on us, but we don't have to adhere to them. There have been many days when I am supposed to be going to the grocery store and for some reason I just can't seem to get moving. Eventually I get out the door and run into someone I haven't seen in years. If I had gotten out the door earlier, I would have missed them! Timing is everything and that is so true.

You are exactly where and when you're supposed to be.

If you know someone who is having this experience—good for you, you can compare notes.

I do not know anyone having a negative experience. Everyone around me, has positive ET experiences. This can be isolating and lonely and you can feel nuts some of the time. But, don't let others' progress or lack affect you. This is not a race. Whenever you discover who and what you are is the right time.

If you have questions, or need help with the tools, feel free to contact me at: lohara@protonmail.com

Resources

Books:

Communion by Whitley Strieber

MILABS: Military Mind Control & Alien Abduction by Dr. Helmut Lammer & Marion Lammer

Incident at Devil's Den, A True Story by Terry Lovelace

Healing Archetypes & Symbols by Stewart A. Swerdlow & Janet Diane Mourglia-Swerdlow

The Hyperspace Helper A User-Friendly Guide by Stewart A. Swerdlow & Janet D. Swerdlow

Access Denied by Cathy O'Brien

Psychic Warrior by David Morehouse

The 7th Sense: The Secrets of Remote Viewing as Told by a "Psychic Spy" for the US Military by Lyn Buchanan

Smeared, No Contact: How to Beat the Narcissist, Fuel, Sitting Target: How and Why the Narcissist Chooses You by H.G. Tudor on narcissism

Groups:

Experiencer On-line Group, Gwen Farrell, etherapist.gf@gmail.com. Email Gwen for details.

Opusnetwork.org

Apps:

App on iPhone App Store: Mediation Oasis by Mary and Richard Maddox

App on iPhone App Store: Yoga Nidra by Kamini Desai, PhD

Helpful Websites:

YouTube: BeGood4000 Channel

Alienjigsaw.com

Etsy.com

Healthsynergyaz.com

Hybridrising.com

Lahochi.com

Narcsite.com

Rockominerals.com

How to Build Your Own Portable Copper Pyramid

Purchase: Four sections of ½" diameter, "M" copper pipes, each piece 5 feet long.

Purchase: 18-Z clear Lamp Wire, 30-35 feet. You will split this apart prior to inserting through the holes of the pipes on bottom. You are making a collapsible pyramid which means the bases cannot be solid copper or otherwise.

Purchase: A 1 ½" key ring (split ring) to hold the pipes together at the top. Maybe buy a couple for spares in case of breakage.

TOP: Mark with a black marker where you'll drill a hole for the top of the pipe. It should be ¼" down from the edge. Then take a hammer and nail to create a small dent in the marked spot. This is to help the drill bit catch on when you start drilling.

Using a drill bit size 3/16: This will be the top of your pyramid where you'll be threading a key ring through.

BOTTOM: Mark a spot ½" from the edge of the bottom pipe and using drill bit size 15/64" do the same thing you did for the top, drill right through the other side. Make sure the bottom hole lines up with the top hole.

Using a pair of pliers, put the key ring through the top holes.

After getting the key ring through the top, you're ready for the last step of the building process. Split apart the wire so you're dealing with a single casing of copper wire rather than double.

Measure out 63.2 inches of wire.

Cut four separate pieces of single casing wire, one for each base. You'll need them to be 6 feet each so that you have at least 6 inches of excess wire on both ends in order to comfortably tie a double knot and cut off any excess wire. Put the wire through the holes and make a knot.

Pyramids open better on carpeted floors. If you have hardwood or other slick floors, get plastic caps for the bottom of your pyramid so that it doesn't slide around or destroy your floors.

Level the Playing Field with Negative ETs Handout

6/29/19

Lisa O'Hara

Negative ETs are narcissists—they twist everything, lie to you, manipulate your emotions, thoughts, etc. Never say the cancellation or Ultimate Protection affirmations out loud.

Loopholes: You've all heard this: "in my highest and best healing, in my best and highest good." This is a loophole. Who decides what is in your highest and best good? You are giving away your power by saying this.

<u>Cancellation</u>: MEMORIZE this affirmation. Never say out LOUD! You must use both sentences each time you use it. You don't need to know if this person/entity is negative or not—let your higher self decide.

- a. Get notebook to write all of your experiences down. Dreams are memories. Write them down too.

- b. Use qualifiers for this tool: anyone, anything, anywhere, any reason new and old <u>fill in the blank</u> make up your own

- c. You will have to be a detective in taking your power back. Use any information you obtain from dreams and if you have a period of time that is blank where they erased your memory, use the *Green Spiral Staircase exercise* in *The Hyperspace Helper* book to remote view to see what happened.

- d. Websites to help you find information to guide you with cancellation: hybridrising.com, Alienjigsaw.com. These sites will have valuable insights in what ETs have been known as negative and what tools they use.

<u>Ultimate Protection</u>: Put your body in this violet triangle, with tetrahedron and octahedron for protection every three days.

This is dangerous. Using these tools will piss off the ETs. Be careful.